THE SANDS OF PIMA ARROYO

AND OTHER ESSAYS

TOM COLE

TABLE OF CONTENTS

THE SANDS OF PIMA ARROYO

ROADS FROM THE SKY—SAND—THE MYSTERIOUS
PYRAMID—STONE HOUSES—DESERT VARNISH—
EXFOLIATION—TEDDY BEAR CHOLLA—CITY LIGHTS—
THE MINE—RELICS—MUTT MITTS—BROKEN GLASS
—"WONDERLUST"—THE WATER TANK—
PETROGLYPHS—RATTLERS—HOT HIKES—BIRDS—THE
RING OF STONES—WASH WALKING—OJO DE AWA—
STILL GREEN ARE MY MEMORIES

There is a mountain south of Phoenix, an exfoliating batholith in a horse latitude, rain shadow desert as hot as any one might find in the world. Its color is brownish and its hills roll off into the distance with little to recommend them to the casual eye. The name of the mountain is simply South Mountain, and it is the biggest city park in the nation.

In 1958, Tempe, Arizona, was bordered by desert, and to the southwest of that desert was the town of Guadalupe, a Yaqui community of contrasting austerity set as is was against the trim, modern city next door. People didn't starve there, but living with no front door on the house was not too far from the norm, and the roofs of many homes were just of chicken-coop tin. The town was a Mexican town, just as Mexican as any south of the border. My parents used to drive us through Guadalupe to go to South Mountain's Pima Canyon, and they used to do this often.

If you have ever flown in a plane over Mexico, you are immediately struck by the very different appearance

1

of the cities from the air as compared to those north of the border, and if you look hard enough, you will know the reason: the roads below are unpaved. So it was with Guadalupe. The streets were made of sand. It wasn't a finely winnowed powder, but a thick-and-thin-grained granite sand devoid of the glittering mica you might find in other parts of the state. The sand flowed down the streets just as it flowed down the arroyos that ran through the hills. It was puffy and dusty and light in color like a sand that had given up the dream of ever really being white. It crunched under the station wagon tires. In the summer, the sand drank up any drop of water until every plant in the town was wilted and seared—or nearly every; here and there a house had a sprinkler going to water a bit of green Bermuda. And a few had the red-blooming bougainvillea, the one plant that would stand stubbornly even when strangled of water. But the rest of the place was sand.

It was through a different country and a different culture that we used to drive when we went down Avenida del Yaqui. At one crossroads, there on the avenue, someone had built a cement pyramid eight feet high. It was the same color as the sand. The pyramid always made its impression upon me as we drove by it, but this was not the place we would turn to drive to Pima Canyon. We made a turn where today no turn exists, and we went on a road that was then much longer than it is today. A new city covers much of the road now, but fifty years ago, you took some time to get to the end, where the roofless, mysterious stone houses stood and the arroyo made its turn through the canyon.

I was a child then, and I would look through the station wagon windows and take in the scenes that somehow shocked and haunted me as we moved deeper into the desert. More than any place I would ever see, South Mountain gave the impression of being very old. On its very face seemed to be painted the passing of time, and on it, too, I could imagine a kind of resignation to that passing. The still scenes of odd, table-shaped boulders and of gravelly stretches of colorless crystals were scenes of a land that had long since given up any resistance to the attrition of the years. The chips of granite were speckled like the retro living room curtains of the 1950s, and the boulders were covered with desert varnish, dark brownish, purplish.

Perhaps the exfoliation of the mountain's rounded boulders and giant slabs of granite further imparted the appearance of great age. It rains but rarely on South Mountain, and so the process was slow, but rainwater, when once it did come down, did what it still does there and everywhere else in the world: it combined with the ground's carbon dioxide and turned to carbonic acid. The acid leeched the feldspar out of the granite so that the crystals of quartz and ferro-magnesians fell about, and the feldspar, converted to clay, found itself blown in the wind to mix with the ever present sand. I didn't know the chemistry then, but I did know that the signs of ruin were everywhere I set my eyes.

And there were the teddy bear cholla too, bright blond on the extremities, but dirty brown under the arms and nearly black up the stalk. There is no dustier, older-looking cactus in the world—and none, by the way, more murderous. Just a brush against it will bring a punishment no careless walker deserves. It was the true jumping cholla. The spiny clumps of cactus, however, did not need the idle touch of some passerby to break away; beneath each plant were piles of them for the coyotes to sidestep, bristling clumps that had fallen on their own. Some glinted with yellow spines, and some were nearly black with a burnt and disintegrated look.

The teddy bear cholla was seen in bajadas, little forests that appeared to have grown in place by having been thrown all together at once down a hillside or across a level stretch of desert. Wherever they landed, they stuck, stopped in mid motion, frozen in place—the whole party of small, but anthropomorphic cacti a snapshot in time. Fifty years later, I would photograph a bajada there and type in the title field of iphoto: Dance of the Cholla.jpg.

We used to stop at the end of the road as there was no way to drive any further. Then we would climb the giant piles of boulders there. We had a name for every special rock and every tunneling crevice that coursed through the pile.

One long slab lying before the pile was eight feet high and fifty feet long. There was space beneath it and openings at both ends, so you could have crawled completely under the stone if not for the pack rats' having stuffed the hollow half full of cholla. Still, I would lie down to look completely under the stone to where I could see the sunlight at the other end. It was a frightening, claustrophobic scene, and I imagined myself for some reason having to make my way under the megalith to the opposite opening fifty feet away.

Sometimes my parents allowed night to fall before we went home. We could hear coyotes and we always listened for a wild cat or a mountain lion though I don't remember if we ever heard either of them. The stars shone bright with the shadow of the mountain upon them and the glow of the capital city on the other side too weak in those days to smudge them away. On the drive back, if you looked to the east anywhere south of Guadalupe, there were no lights at all.

On the days that we spent an afternoon there, we sometimes walked up the arroyo. Table-like slabs of stone jutted out from its banks, ready for any of us to set with silverware and place chair in front of. But we never did—and we didn't walk far up the wash either. A hundred yards along we knew there was an old mine blasted into the hill, but we only went there once or twice to see the evidence of copper: a thin green coating of malachite on the occasional stone, barely pretty enough to take home as a souvenir.

In our youth, although we were brimming with energy, that energy was not boundless; it had very strict restrictions that governed its use: to wit, it could only be used in play. A simple walk to the mine was looked upon by the puerile body and soul as drudgery no less painful than the almost physically incapacitating encumbrance of taking out the trash. We preferred climbing the rocks and running ourselves to exhaustion to the toil of walking up Pima Arroyo. We'd squeeze ourselves through the tunneling crevices in the mountain of stones or slide a thousand times over a favorite granite ridge into the arroyo. Once, I slid down the ridge so many times that I found that I had simply worn the seat from my pants, and I was sick with mortification with no change of clothes in the midst of the family's picnic guests.

Today I still go to the same place by the stone houses where I tore my pants. A few years ago, a park ranger on a horse showed me Indian petroglyphs there five feet from the pants-tearing ridge. The scene on the stone was carved through the manganese oxide desert varnish as are most such etchings—only this petroglyph depicted a group of dancing stick figures holding hands. It was a rock drawing much more light-hearted than the usual stoic themes one saw on the mountain: man, whorl, bighorn sheep, etc. I didn't tell the ranger that I surely would have remembered the figures if they had been there when I was a child. And I didn't tell him that I doubted that the ancient Native Americans were in the habit of dancing around holding hands because they never carved such scenes into rock as far as I knew. I did know that just below the carvings were a dozen coyote skulls—the remains of some sheepherder's ghastly slaughter—buried in the sand. We found them there decades ago while digging a barbecue pit—and we reinterred them.

The stone houses were the stopping place of many who came to Pima Canyon, and there by the pile of stones and the granite ridge were the signs of these visitors. Most everywhere you looked were the brown shards of broken beer bottles and the ground was scattered thick with spent .22 shells. The whole area glinted Budweiser brown. Even in the 1980s, bottle breaking and shooting were common at the end of the road, but sometime later, there was a drastic change. The park became more carefully managed, and if you found a piece of glass, it was a relic of the past—just as are the now rare, old rusted beer cans with the triangular church key punch holes. When I find one out in the desert, I look upon it with a kind of joy and treat it as an antique to leave in place as part of Arizona's legacy. I find such treasures still—the old miner's bean can with a peeled back top or a sardine can rusted for a hundred years lying under a bush with its lid rolled neatly around the key that has been carefully tucked inside. And occasionally I find a far more ancient item like a Hohokam chipping stone made of basalt.

How the city could have rid the area of all of those bullet shells and broken bottles is a mystery to me. I think of Darwin's study on earthworms and how long it took them to bury the flints in his field. Even without any earthworms in the desert to cover the pieces of broken bottle, the entire park is today surprisingly glass free, and the trails, though walked by people in the hundreds, show almost no sign of litter. In recent years, there has been a change of mindset and culture; the hikers of today simply pack out what they pack in. The only occasional exception is the fault of the dog owners. The city provides bags for dog dew called "Mutt Mitts," and people pack these bags in. Unfortunately, once used for their intended purpose, they are not especially pleasing to pack out, and so you will sometimes see one lying plump on the side of a road or trail where it has been left by an insufficiently principled and less than stalwart walker.

Let me tell you of a littering incident. I was making a cross-country expedition in a remote area of the park when I saw that someone had left a movie ticket on the ground. As most people would, I reflected that the person should have been more careful with such trash. I looked at the ticket and it said, "Fahrenheit 911, June 26, 2004." When I got home, on a hunch I searched Pima Canyon in my bird database. There, I found a page for the same date with a note about the matinee I had gone to just before the hike. It was I who had been the litterer.

It goes to show why I have the database. Consider my visit to the dentist the other day. The technician tried to convince me that I was having my sixth crown. "But I only have two right now," I protested." She got out a mirror and we looked in my mouth and counted five. There is no way for the human mind to track all of these crowns or hikes—or trips even just to one place like Pima Canyon. Yet the human soul (or at least mine) yearns to know how many hikes there have been and when they were. Paper records are good, but they don't compare to the database—as it can be searched in a wink—and as far as the bird list goes, I, myself, can sort any specific finch from all of the flocks of sparrows and finches I have ever seen at Pima Canyon, anywhere else, or everywhere else.

The computer age that I scoffed at as a twenty-year-old has changed life for the better. For me, a large part of life used to be a dreary journey of what I call "unrequited wonder lust." In the past, you might wish to check where and when you went and be stymied by a yard-high stack of moldy notebooks. Coming home from a hike when the wonder lust hit you, you would not perhaps have the energy to leaf through them all to check for what you wanted to know unless your reference system was particularly well thought-out. And with regard to other facts, you may have wished to learn, there was much you would have trouble finding even in a library. Remember those old rocket radios? They were simple crystal radios you could buy for a dollar fifty. You pulled the nose cone up to change channels, and there was an alligator clip to hook to a window screen or other piece of metal as an antennae. In the 80s I could only imagine what they used to look like and wished I could see one again. Today, not only can I see a picture of one, I can buy one in its original box on Ebay. In 1968, the Smothers Brothers read a poem on their show, and for years I wanted to have a copy, but I would have had to ask the librarian if she remembered it—which was unlikely, and they wouldn't have a copy anyway. Now I Google it.

Life is abundant.

But my trips to Pima Canyon are not on the internet; they're on my intranet and I wonder no more about anything that has happened. A few years ago, I was surfing my intranet and found that I had no record for a trip to Pima Canyon in the year 2000. I remembered that I had hurt my leg bird watching on Kentucky Derby Day around the year 2000 at Elliot and Cooper Roads. I knew that it took a year to heal, and so for a while, my reality was that my missed trips to the canyon were because of my leg. In subsequent surfing, I found that I hurt my leg in 2001. Later, when I integrated my journal and bird database, I happened to find a year 2000 trip that was not in the bird database, so I took the opportunity to put it in there where it belonged with no bird sighting associated with it. There seems to be just one trip in 2000. I don't know why that is, but I do know it isn't because of my leg.

In the spring of 2004, I stepped down from my eight-year position as the Associate Director of the program for which I worked at Arizona State University. I had longed for a summer vacation for many years and was able to get six weeks off before I returned to the teaching faculty. I did not waste the vacation. Every day for that time, I would get up and work on a grammar book and software project of mine. And after the morning's work, I would head to South Mountain and hike up the arroyo. A click or two in my database shows that I went twenty-eight times to the canyon in June, July, and August:

SUMMER 2004 TRIPS TO PIMA CANYON

1. Pima Canyon,06/05/2004,Birds: 7,Total ever: 471
2. Pima Canyon,06/06/2004,Birds: 10,Total ever: 481
3. Pima Canyon,06/13/2004,Birds: 7,Total ever: 488
4. Pima Canyon,06/19/2004,Birds: 8,Total ever: 496
5. Pima Canyon,06/20/2004,Birds: 16,Total ever: 512
6. Pima Canyon,06/26/2004,Birds: 6,Total ever: 518
7. Pima Canyon,06/27/2004,Birds: 17,Total ever: 535
8. Pima Canyon,07/01/2004,Birds: 9,Total ever: 544
9. Pima Canyon,07/02/2004,Birds: 10,Total ever: 554
10. Pima Canyon,07/03/2004,Birds: 6,Total ever: 560
11. Pima Canyon,07/04/2004,Birds: 7,Total ever: 567
12. Pima Canyon,07/05/2004,Birds: 5,Total ever: 572

13. Pima Canyon,07/06/2004,Birds: 8,Total ever: 580
14. Pima Canyon,07/08/2004,Birds: 6,Total ever: 586
15. Pima Canyon,07/15/2004,Birds: 5,Total ever: 591
16. Pima Canyon,07/19/2004,Birds: 5,Total ever: 596
17. Pima Canyon,07/21/2004,Birds: 6,Total ever: 602
18. Pima Canyon,07/22/2004,Birds: 5,Total ever: 607
19. Pima Canyon,07/27/2004,Birds: 4,Total ever: 611
20. Pima Canyon,07/28/2004,Birds: 4,Total ever: 615
21. Pima Canyon,07/30/2004,Birds: 3,Total ever: 618
22. Pima Canyon,07/31/2004,Birds: 5,Total ever: 623
23. Pima Canyon,08/01/2004,Birds: 2,Total ever: 625
24. Pima Canyon,08/02/2004,Birds: 2,Total ever: 627
25. Pima Canyon,08/03/2004,Birds: 3,Total ever: 630
26. Pima Canyon,08/11/2004,Birds: 3,Total ever: 633
27. Pima Canyon,08/13/2004,Birds: 3,Total ever: 636
28. Pima Canyon,08/29/2004,Birds: 5,Total ever: 641

On most of these days, I would walk up to the water tank and back on the stone road. The water tank drained into a small, square cement reservoir that held water for thirsty javelinas, coyotes, and other desert animals. I call the top stone that overlooks the arroyo there "Windy Rock" as there always seems to be a cool, welcome breeze when you climb up and stand on it. Below, the arroyo is wired off, and signs are posted that read "Wildlife Area"—but the real reason I expect is to protect the petroglyphs and corn grinding holes on the rock below. One petroglyph, a humanoid stick figure, is said to be cut across by a ray of sunlight at the winter solstice. The figure seems to be saluting, but my brother gave a better interpretation of the figure. "He's shading his eyes from the winter sun," he said.

Occasionally, a coyote would walk by and look at me bored and unsociable. He would walk out of the wash and up into the desert to avoid me. But there were dangerous animals there too; to be specific: rattlesnakes. In the heat of the summer, they are not likely out and about, unless they are in a cool patch of shade under a bush, but when spring comes and they come out of hibernation, they can be anywhere. Of the four kinds that I have seen there, the most common is especially dangerous: the tiger rattler. It has a mixture of a cobra-like neurotoxin and the standard rattler's flesh-eating enzyme. This cocktail of poisons is something I want no part of.

The weather on these summer hikes was exceedingly hot, but that was the reason I went. In the summer, the park is deserted before noon; it just gets too hot for the average hiker. There are, however, hot hikers, and I am one of them.

My college roommate, some years ago had taken up hiking because he had grown rather overweight and needed to exercise, so I took to joining him on various desert hikes. When the season turned cooler, we both agreed that we missed the hot weather's challenge, the sweaty workout, and the cool, sparkling drinks we brought along. Afterwards, I noticed that when I hiked in the blazing heat of an Arizona summer day, I would find, say, a middle-aged woman sitting on the sand in Pima Arroyo when it was 114° in the shade. Or I would climb into "the tunnel," a natural rock formation three miles in, and find that a happy hiker had beat me there and was already more versed than I in the practice of hot hiking. "Everybody's gone by eleven o'clock in the summer, and you've got the place to yourself." he said.

I had to agree with him. Who wants to go anywhere in nature when there are a lot of people around—especially in a place where you are so grandfathered in that sometimes you can't help but feel that the rest of the world is trespassing?

The idea of hot hiking is not to suffer but to beat the heat. I carry bottles of fizzy, flavored water and a platypus bottle filled with ice water. They say that in times of crisis, one must never waste water by doing anything with it other than drinking it, but on my hikes I have plenty of fizzy water, and if I feel hot, I take the icy platypus water and pour it over my head. When you're super hydrated from the fizzy water and practically freezing to death at the same time, you're in more danger of catching a cold than dying of heatstroke. I admit to having come close to danger when I decided to climb a steep trail in the heat. Working up a sweat and overheating from strenuous exercise is not a good idea, and I'm extra careful today; on February 11, 2006, I took a group of Korean scholars to Old Tucson Studios, and one of them got heat stroke watching the gunfights in the street. It was only 85 degrees, and I thought she would die.

In the heat of the summer, the walk up Pima Arroyo is quiet and still. Mourning doves, seemingly unaffected by the temperature, walk quietly in the shade under the creosote bushes. When you approach too close, they take to flight, but even the usual whistling sound of their wings on takeoff seems to have been almost silenced. I hesitate to say this is because of the superheated air.

Passenger jets pass, but they are still at good altitude and rarely heard. Only birds regularly break the silence of the hot hike. You will occasionally hear the chish! chish! chish! chish! of the giant cactus wren. Around one of the bends in the wash is "Cactus Wren Alley." Whenever I hike with a guest, I tell them what bird we will expect to see there by the turn in the arroyo with the steep cliffs on one side—and we see exactly that. Not just one, but rarely fewer than three at once.

The scolding cry of the black-tailed gnatcatcher, a tiny, intrepid bird of the desert and the bell-like call of the black-throated sparrow are also heard. Because of their names and their presence there, I named one area of the arroyo "the BT Cliffs." I always make a silent approach when I seen the cliffs, as not only the two BTs like the cool, shady, brushy bluffs there but also the gilded flicker and a half dozen other species. And you may see all of them there at once.

The road back to the car is downhill. One doesn't notice the slight uphill climb up the wash, but this combined with the heavy, tiring sand makes the first half of the hike harder. There's more cooling wind on the road too, although there is no shade at all.

A quarter mile from the parking lot is a ring of stones in the middle of the road. Fifty years ago, I would look ahead of the car to see it, and today I do much the same as I walk—only it is barely visible now. The stones are buried, and their tops are flush with the surface of the road. As do all rings of stone, they foster in me a sense of mysticism. Who put the ring of stones there? What was it? A campfire? Just for fun, I have taken to doing a kind of war dance on the stones before I go any farther. Sometimes I stuff a bottle of Boston Lager at the bottom of the pack in an ice-filled ziplock bag, and I drink it on the ring of stones as part of the ritual.

The trip to the water tank doesn't even get you as far as the stone houses, but there are endless miles of trails that lead you away from the more populated, scarred areas near the road: Mormon Trail, National Trail, and others that take you to Fat Man's Pass, Hidden Valley, the Tunnel, and other places. On days when my friends and I plan a miles-long hike, we often skip the trails for the first half of the walk and continue up Pima Arroyo and come back on the trails. Few people do this wash walking, so you've got it to yourself even early in the day. And it is as wild and pristine as you could imagine a place so close to the city. The saguaros are tall and stately there, and there is almost no sign of man. Painted letters on one cliff used to read: Ojo de Awa, misspelled Spanish for "well." An arrow pointed to a depression in the sandy ground below. A few years ago, that part of the cliff fell off, and the words can no longer be read. I'm sure I have a picture somewhere of it—but the picture was not digital, and so I will have to rumble through some old boxes if I ever get the urge to see it again.

When I go up the arroyo, I always climb the dry falls where the granite is fluted as though carved by a sculptor to make way for the occasional rush of a flash flood's water. And then I walk a little farther and find myself in Hidden Valley not far from Fat Man's Pass and the Tunnel. Sometimes I skip the arroyo entirely and take a trail clear to the top and walk along the long ridges on the crest of the mountain with the cheerful view of Phoenix below.

There are other places that I know as well: Estero de Morua, Mexico, for example, or our hacienda at the foot of Mount Humphrey's. Many, too, were the days that I spent on the shores of Minnesota's pristine Lake Itasca, and still green are the memories of my summers there. But more often now I find myself thinking about South Mountain and the sands of Pima Arroyo. I see the mountain when I walk out of my front gate, when I go to the store, and when I drive home from work.

I've paid off my house now, and there is little reason to relocate when I retire; I could hardly expect to find a place to live where I could find anything with the uniqueness of the Sonoran Desert so close at hand or a place that captured my imagination in the way it does. I still travel back to Mexico and Minnesota and even more often drive up to stay at our acres at the foot of Mount Humphrey's. But my everyday life is likely to be forever based in this placid, convenient Valley suburb, and South Mountain is a good thing to always have so close-by.

How the Cowboys Lost Their Hats

The Magic Spring—The Realization—Who among
Us Can Forget the Disparaging Remarks?—A
Willful New Path to a Bright New Destiny—
Kinder, Gentler Cowboys—Burning Their
Agricultural Draft Deferments—Lonely
Cowboys—A Bull Cowgirl—A Crate Of
Horseshoes—Feelings of Sexual Inadequacy—
The Literate Rejoinder—A Shout of Judgment—
The Amnesia of Our New Times

It was late in the spring of 1973 and the cowboys
were about to lose their hats. The evidence was
everywhere—evidence that seemed so very plain and
obvious to me as I breathed the thick, intoxicating air of
the approaching magic summer. The change was
coming. You couldn't miss it if you tried, and it was
very fine to know that it was finally—finally
happening! In my enthusiasm, I spoke of it excitedly to
my friends and neighbors. I said, "Look, everyone—
look! The cowboys are losing their hats!"

But no one took notice. They did not believe that
such a thing could be, and it is only now that history
has born out the truth of my words that the doubters
must admit that it happened exactly as I said it would.
And who today could deny it?

I watched it start slowly when first the cowboys'
hair sprouted bushily and began pushing—literally
pushing the hats off their heads. I didn't know what it

17

meant at first, for I was confused. Were these not the same cowboys who shouted their angry insults at the very sight of the long-haired young men of the time? Who among us can forget the disparaging and emasculating terms they used? And now there were to be long-haired cowboys? Here was something very new and something wonderful—wonderful because of what it meant. And it meant that here were cowboys who would not—could not—yell what they had always yelled before. It meant that the cowboys had willfully—willfully mind you—chosen a new path in life that did not include the angry insults. Here were cowboys who knew what they were giving up to do this and cowboys who were doing it anyhow—kinder, gentler cowboys who had made an overture—and made it on their own —to join their brethren, burn their agricultural draft deferments and let the dim past be forgotten. They were cowboys not afraid to be in touch with their feminine side—real trailblazing American cowboys who had made a giant leap towards a bright new destiny.

Oh, the cowboys weren't always as you know them today. So often before I had seen them: lonely cowboys —lonely in their own company for even as they hurled their homophobic invective they knew as everyone else that there was never a girl in their midst. Never. Not in the saloons where the cowboys gathered young and gangly around the tables for beer. Not in their pick-up trucks with the gun racks and the peace sign bumper stickers labeled "Footprint of the American Chicken." Not in the chow line nor sitting with them on the corral fence on those unmatched spring days or visiting the bunkhouse on those priceless and irreplaceable spring evenings. But I am unfair, for in reality there was one woman present in every cowboy gathering. A stern and masculine woman was she—a bale-hurling girlie-man who would give you a woolly look and yell, "Is that a guy or a gal!" in her coarse cigarette voice as the cowboys twenty strong went, "Yuck, yuck, yuck!" and, often as not, "Duh!" She was there with them as you will recall, but I'm not sure whether she ever lost her hat. And I'm not sure that she even stayed there with the cowboys to witness their brave Metamorphosis.

As news of the sexual revolution became old news, the cowboys realized that they had not been footnoted in this part of history. One day, in a sublime moment of clarity, this fact hit the cowboys like a crate of horseshoes. And it hurt. To solace themselves, they took to putting bumper stickers on their pick-ups that read, "Cowboys Make Better Lovers." But the façade was too transparent. They weren't fooling anyone and the hippie men weren't about to let them get away with it either—not after having been called "faggot" umpteen thousand times. No sir. The next day dawned clear and bright, and every VW Microbus in the country had a sticker on it that read, "Cowboys Suffer From Feelings of Sexual Inadequacy."

The retort struck home and its unvarnished truth was too much for the cowboys. Reeling beneath their hats, hopelessly outclassed and overwhelmed by the sheer power of the hippies' simple, literate rejoinder, the cowboys reassessed the situation, reconnoitered, and decided to cut their losses by removing the stickers the very next day. And at once the hippies responded in kind. A day later, you could look at any microbus from

Maine to Albuquerque, from Taos to Bisbee, from Flagstaff clean to Klamath Falls and there was no sign that the fierce rebuttal had ever been penned and plastered there. "You don't beat a man when he's down," was the hippies' reasoning. "Wage peace."

Miraculously this was not lost on the cowboys. They mulled it over—this reciprocal overture to them—and they continued their historic transformation and reformation. They carried on with what was surely the most remarkable pilgrimage of introspection ever embarked upon.

The cowboys began to learn things they had never known before. They met new people. Soon the cowboys saw, yet dimly, that there were other lives that people led—different lives from theirs, but somehow inextricably linked to theirs. Sometimes, they found it was fun to revel in their differences—more fun and rewarding by far than shouting hurtful names at those who were somehow different.

Once, in the Palomino Club, I sat as one new to the company of cowboys, a hippie losing his hair. The TV blared above the bar and on it suddenly appeared the specter of the police beating an African American man. It was ten against one, and the clubs rained down. I dare not guess what the unreconstructed cowboy might have said at this sight. All I heard, however, were the words of one slow-drawling buckaroo who shook his head and said, "Hell's bells. You don't beat a man when he's down."

Yes, the cowboys were learning and they were growing, but they had not entirely lost their hats. Not yet.

The cowboys could still be seen in the airport waiting gates when they traveled, sporting their biggest hats and jawing and alolligagging and laying it all on just too, too daggunned thick. Each cowboy was still too often attending his own private masquerade ball and that would have to change. And change it did when law enforcement cowboys somehow got permission to wear their hats on the job.

The cowboy cops were naive and unsophisticated and they thought that the hats would please the public. They thought they were providing a bit of welcome western color for all to share. But the public had no urge to fantasize that they lived in Dodge City. They were practical, hardworking folk and to them the hats carried an entirely different connotation—one that they just plain didn't like. They had all seen In the Heat of the Night with Sidney Poitier and Rod Steiger, and they weren't about to brook any nonsense in their town from any redneck cowboy cops who didn't have the common horse sense to get rid of their hats before there was trouble.

The disapproval was directed at the hats and it was nation-wide. Anger and resentment grew and the cowboys were but faintly aware of it. When at last it came pouring out in a collective American shout of judgment, the cowboys were unprepared, and yet the message was loud and clear even to them and they knew what they must do.

The cowboy cops attempted to work and people would roll down their car windows and shout the message. When the cowboys drove their trucks, people gathered at the roadside to give the battle cry. There was no escaping it, and the words of simple and unrefined disapproval were always the same. They were, "Nice hat, *JACKASS!*"

And as if by magic at these words, there was a mystical whooshing sound as the hats were swept from the cowboys' heads. And along with the hats went the gun racks and the intolerance and all the rest that had kept the cowboys from living out their destinies as the true American Cowboys they were meant to be.

Whoosh! went the hats across the eastern seaboard over the Adirondacks. *Whoosh!* across the South. *Whoosh! Whoosh!* went the hats from the Iowa corn land to the lake country of Minnesota. *Whoosh!* over the Great Plains and over the still, checkered fields and the great granite mountains and the green valleys and the sandstone canyons and the diamond deserts!

The transformation that day was at last complete. The cowboys had fulfilled their quest.

I suppose there are more important dates in the history of our great nation—more important turning points: our first day of independence, the close of the Civil War, D-Day, the day that Kennedy died, the day the Beatles invaded our shores. But there is none so undeservedly shrouded and forgotten in the amnesia of our new times as the day the cowboys lost their hats.

LUCKY

This story has no ending—at least it won't until
Lucky dies. But he just keeps on living and living. All
of the other pigeons in the old coop have been dead ten,
twenty years, and I've long given up raising birds
though I've still got Lucky. He's half white and half
what we call ash-red. His feet don't work well though
he can stand and waddle a bit. But I can fly a lot better
than he can now. He just sits there in the little cage on
the kitchen floor. Sometimes he coos. Sometimes he
growls. Mostly he just sits there. Out in the back yard is
the old, empty pigeon coop. We used to write notes in
pencil on the back of the coop whenever a pigeon
hatched. It was a lousy record system; the boards
weathered and the writing faded and finally vanished
entirely, so I don't know Lucky's exact date of hatch.
But he's twenty-three years old if he's a day.

Pinned to my kitchen bulletin board is my brother's
cancelled check for $20.94. It is dated August 3, 1985
and made out to "Roer's Bird Farm." That was the
check he and I used to buy Lucky's parents along with
another pair or two. I tend to keep things: old checks,
my baby teeth, Lucky.

We had the worst time getting those birds to breed.
The eggs wouldn't hatch, and we tossed them out well
before the 21-day gestation period was over as they

23

were obviously rotten. But finally, Speckles, Lucky's mother, laid a single egg that actually hatched and we named the squab Lucky.

Afterwards, the pigeons reproduced like crazy, and the coop would get so full that we'd take thirty or so at a time down to the zoo and let them go. We never got rid of Lucky because he was the first to hatch. There were lots of other pigeons to which we had sentimental attachment, and they stayed home too: Squeaky, Mohawk, Cielito.

The zoo was not really the best place for the birds we exiled, but it was far enough away that they wouldn't fly back home like racing homers.

We really thought they stood a fighting chance of eking out a living at the zoo or we wouldn't have dumped them there. And we didn't look upon their banishment as certain death even though we knew the zookeepers had a big "pigeon net." They would sometimes throw it across a couple of hundred feeding pigeons at a time and then serve the birds they caught to the wildcats and other animals that needed fresh meat.

We used to fly our pigeons in those days. They would "kit up" in a group and fly straight above the house so high that we could hardly see them. Then, being rollers, they would roll. Well, not Lucky. He wasn't such a good roller.

I said that we were fond of some of the birds and over the years the one to which I had the greatest sentimental attachment was Twizzie. I had him when I was eight or nine years old and kept him in a different coop in the backyard of a different house long before the days of Lucky, and Speckles, and Cielito.

Twizzie was a gentle soul and the best pigeon I ever owned. I named him Twizzie because he didn't roll but twizzled, did back flips instead of rolling. Twizzie, like Lucky, was a roller and as such was supposed to fly to good altitude and roll backwards straight down thirty feet or more and recover. The deep rolling breeds, the Birmingham or Pensom rollers did just that, but it was also a hazardous habit because if a bird rolled too far, it would hit the ground and die. Twizzie's mate, a blue check hen, hit the roof of our house on a roll and was knocked out cold. We put her in a recovery cage, and she finally woke up and was put back in the coop. She survived for many years, but never rolled again. Ever.

I used to take Twizzie to school with me and release him out on the playground. He'd circle and do back flips before heading home with the flash of his white wing tips contrasting against his dark body. Sometimes I'd go out for recess and see him high up in the sky flying and doing flips. I loved everything about Twizzie —even his coo was the perfect pigeon coo: Guadalupe, Guadalupe...

Twizzie got run over by the irrigation man's truck. It came as a blow to me. As I said, Twizzie was a gentle soul and the best pigeon I ever owned.

MATING FOR LIFE—A POPULATION DROP—PAINTED ON THEIR PERCHES—DREAMS OF FLIGHT—SQUEAKY AND CHALKY—THE MAUSOLEUM—VLADIMIR LENIN

Pigeons mate for life, but they are still a little promiscuous, and if their mate is gone any time at all, they quickly mate for life again. Lucky's mate of many years died and he then said, "I do" to Speckles, who was his mother, but what do pigeons know or care? He sired countless offspring that either died of old age, wound up getting fed to wildcats, or flew the coop some other way.

Playing host to all of these pigeons became tiresome over the years, and so I kept my favorites, and in time they became infertile, and the population began to drop in the coop as they died. I never did let them out to fly again.

I remember seeing two of them, Columbus and Cielito year after year sitting still upon their perches as though painted there. They rarely moved. It gave me a pang of guilt every time I looked at them.

But I was always able to solace myself with the memory of what happened to a rough and tumble old street pigeon I invited to the coop. He became the cock o' the walk immediately and loved the place. In the coop, he had a social life, three squares, and no cat trouble. I once tried to throw him out of the coop, and he flew back and clung to the chicken wire, desperate to be caged again. I gave him his wish.

Pigeons love the coop, but still I wondered if these old birds sometimes dreamed of flying once more. Somehow, I'm sorry to say, I believe they always did. How could they not?

Squeaky was a petite blue bar roller with splashes of white on her face. I was fond of her, and she fell into a very elite group of pigeons along with Twizzie and one old cull I remember named Chalky. They were special because they were so obviously smarter than all of the other pigeons. They'd trick you when you'd open the door and make a break for it, getting right past you and taking to the sky. Squeaky did this quite often and I would shout, "Get back here, Squeaky!" And wouldn't you know it, Squeaky would fly back and dive right through the door again and alight on her perch. She knew exactly what I said—or so it seemed at least to me.

Squeaky got sick and died, and I froze her in the refrigerator, which has become something of a pigeon mausoleum. As I said, I tend to keep things, and for those who think this is a strange habit, I point out that Vladimir Lenin has been lying in state wearing the same cheap suit for close to a hundred years with (as far as I know) no refrigeration at all, and people wait in line just to see.

CHUCKLES—PECKING—DARWIN'S PIGEONS—MENDEL —GENETICS—NEO PROFESSORS—THE DILUTE GENE

One day, more than ten years ago, Chuckles came to the coop. One of the women at work had a pigeon and she asked me if I would adopt it, and I did, and I regretted it.

You see, Chuckles brought with her a kind of vileness and wickedness that I don't remember seeing very often in a coop. Oh, the coop can be plenty tough even without a bird like Chuckles. The walls at the floor of the coop, for example, should always have a kind of running board, a wooden skirt a few inches above the floor, so any squabs that might happen to fall out of the nest can get under it and not be pecked to death. And yes, once, my brother was examining a

27

squab and then accidentally put him into the wrong nest box, and the pair of birds living there pecked it until there was nothing but a pink skull cap showing. In the case of skull peckings, by the way, there was never an infection. The squab would slowly heal and skin would cover the bared bone. Afterwards, down would grow until perhaps three years later the adult bird would have a smoothly feathered head like a bird that had never been scalped at all.

Yes, there were some rough moments in the coop. Still, Chuckles was to bring with her a ferocity and meanness that I have rarely seen in a bird, especially a hen.

Now, Chuckles didn't come with a name. When my father saw the bird, he said, "Why don't you name him Charles Darwin?" Chuck for short. Well, I had a Columbus, so a historic name wasn't out of the question. We thought Chuck was a cock at first (You can only tell the gender by the bird's behavior.), so we didn't know we'd have to change the name to Chuckles, only slightly more feminine in sound. But I knew that Darwin was a good person to name a bird after, being as he was the most famous of all pigeon fanciers. In fact, he kicked off his first chapter of The Origins of Species with:

"Believing that it is always best to study some special group, I have, after deliberation, taken up domestic pigeons. I have kept every breed which I could purchase or obtain and have been most kindly favored with skins from several quarters of the world... Many treatises in different languages have been published on pigeons and some of them are very important, as being of considerable antiquity. I have associated with several eminent fanciers, and have been permitted to join two of the London Pigeon Clubs."

They talk about Darwin's finches, but perhaps it was really his pigeons that are to credit for his insights. The pigeon was absolutely perfect for the development of Darwin's theory. He knew that the breeds of pigeon were so preposterously different in appearance that no sane person could place half of them in the same genus by their morphology alone—much less call them the same species. There were giant "runts" with three-foot wingspans, broken-necked fantails, sliver-thin tipplers, chicken-like modenas, pug-faced Chinese "owls," and falcon-winged Ukrainian sky cutters. And yet all scientists and fanciers universally agreed that they were all simply variations of the common rock dove, *Columba livia*—not because anyone knew a single thing about genetics at the time, but because they could all make babies together.

Darwin devised a wonderful experiment which perhaps is best to let him explain himself as he did in the first chapter of *The Origin of Species*:

> I crossed some white fantails, which breed very true, with some black barbs—and so it happens that blue varieties of barbs are so rare that I never heard of an instance in England; and the mongrels were black, brown, and mottled. I also crossed a barb with a spot, which is a white bird with a red

tail and red spot on the forehead, and which notoriously breeds very true; the mongrels were dusky and mottled. I then crossed one of the mongrel barb-fantails with a mongrel barb-spot, and they produced a bird of as beautiful and blue colour, with the white loins, double black wing bar, and barred and white-edged tail-feathers, as any wild-rock pigeon!

In short, the barb-spot-fantail mix reverted back to a classic blue bar street pigeon with no effort at selection on Darwin's part. It would be hard not to wonder how great a part this experiment may have played in Darwin's work on diversity and evolution.

Now, here we come to genetics, an advantage that contemporary breeders have over Darwin. Let me explain this advantage with the following story: there was a department head at a major university who was kind of deranged and used to hire only Baptist preachers to teach biology. This may sound like an outrageous claim, and it's one my father used to make, but consider this: my mom came up to me once and said, "Tom last night Jerry was introduced to a biology professor whose wife said he'd been hired by W.T. Wentworth. Jerry shouted, 'Well you must be a Baptist preacher!' and his wife said, 'Er... actually he is.' " *Faux pas* City, but my father couldn't have cared less, and it does show there was some truth to his claim.

At any rate, the story goes that these neo-professors would get up and have the undergraduates take notes as they said various things. One of the things they always said was "If Darwin had known about Gregor Mendel, he would never have developed his theory of evolution." The undergraduates would write these words down in their notebooks and carefully review them later. Then, there would be a test.

In actuality, though, Darwin would have loved to have known about his contemporary Mendel because he could have explained, in part, the problem people confronted him with regarding the selection of favored characteristics in plant and animal populations. People argued that advantageous genes of a particularly sturdy animal would simply find themselves awash in the run-of-the mill genes of its mate—diluted like watered-down whiskey generation after generation until there was no whiskey left at all, just a homeopathic remedy of some sort. There was no mechanism, they argued, to keep the favored characteristics from being very quickly winnowed away. I imagine Darwin might have replied to this with something like, "So you envision a system in which all the genes just average out and we are all stuck with the lowest common denominator— repeatedly. Well, that would appear to be true, but since this doesn't describe the real world, and I am obviously correct in this by all the evidence, we can only assume that there may be somewhere an Austrian monk named Gregor Mendel, whose fledgling science of genetics will begin to explain some of this with its dominant and recessive genes and so on."

Darwin would have liked Mendel's work for a better reason than that it upheld his theory; he would have liked it for the sheer fun it provides the pigeon fancier. For example, Darwin would have liked to know about

31

the dilute gene that turned his blue birds to silver and his red ones to yellow. When Lucky hatched, we immediately knew by his thick coat of yellow down that he would not be a "dilute" with regard to color. Birds with the dilute gene hatch naked.

The dilute gene is recessive and sex linked. Pigeons have no Y chromosome, and the male has two X's and the female just one. I used to write a zero next to the female's single X for purposes of symmetry and clarity when I mapped things out: X0 is a hen, and XX is a cock. Since the dilute gene is recessive, a male will need two of them for the dilute color trait to show up in his appearance—his phenotype. The following chart shows how an otherwise XX red cock becomes diluted to a cool-looking yellow when the dilute gene (indicated by a little "d") is present on both X chromosomes, and how in the same way a blue cock becomes silver:

Adding Two Recessive, Sex-Linked Dilute Genes to Both X Chromosomes

XX = Red Cock or Xd Xd = Yellow Cock
XX = Blue Cock or Xd Xd = Silver Cock

The female with a dilute gene always shows the trait in her phenotype because the recessive gene has only that zero to compete with it. Thus, using a zero to even things out for the missing Y chromosome, an otherwise X0 red hen becomes a cool-looking yellow bird when the dilute gene is present on the X chromosome, and a blue hen becomes silver.

> **Adding One Recessive, Sex-Linked Dilute Gene to the X Chromosome**
>
> $X0$ = Red Hen or $X^d 0$ = Yellow Hen
>
> $X0$ = Blue Hen or $X^d 0$ = Silver Hen

Some males carry the trait but do not show it. In that case, if you cross a male carrier with a non-diluted female, you can sometimes know the sex of a squab the minute it hatches. It's easy. Any of their offspring that hatch naked will be females—and will show the dilute color trait when they grow feathers.

> **Female Parent + Male Parent (Carrier)**
> $X0$ XdX
>
> **FOUR POSSIBLE KINDS OF OFFSPRING**
>
> | Females | | Males | |
> |---|---|---|---|
> | 25% | 25% | 25% | 25% |
> | $X0$ | $Xd0$ | XX | XdX |
> | No Dilute Gene | Shows Trait | No Dilute Gene | Carries Trait |

There's a world of genetics like this and breeders have fun mapping out whether the birds will be barred or checked or grizzled or whatever.

The Story of Chica, An Unsettling tale—Nearly Beheaded—Timeshare—Banishment—The Ants Always Know

When Chuckles went into the coop, Lucky had no mate as Speckles had died, so Lucky and Chuckles paired up. By this time Lucky was infertile, and so Chuckles would lay infertile eggs, and I would end up breaking them after a time, and Chuckles would lay more. In a short time, the last of the other pigeons in the coop died, and Lucky and Chuckles had the place to themselves.

One day, I was driving home through a kind of run-down neighborhood and saw a pigeon with a broken wing. For some reason I stopped, picked him, up and put him in the car. The neighborhood was heavily Hispanic, so I named him Chico and later Chica when I found that he was a she.

Chica went into the coop and went on living. Years passed and one day I saw that Chuckles wouldn't allow Chica to eat. Chuckles had a new nest on the floor and that's where I threw the grain, so Chuckles was defending the whole floor as her nest. Chica, with her maimed wing, was no match for Chuckles, yet the trouble seemed to pass, and I soon forgot all about Chuckles' attacking Chica.

One day, I found Chica on the floor of the coop apparently dead. I picked her up and found she was breathing. I felt she was on her last legs, so I took her to the side yard and got a shovel to cut off her head, but I lost my nerve and called my brother. "Hey, Steve," I said. "Will you come over and cut this pigeon's head off? I can't stand to do it."

"No," he answered "*Hell*, no. Do it yourself."

I went back to Chica with the shovel and pressed it against her neck ready in an instant to slam it down and put her out of her misery. I tried again and again, but I couldn't force myself to do it. Finally, I chickened out entirely and got a little cage from behind the coop and put Chica in it. I put the cage and the bird in the kitchen. The next morning, Chica was standing up looking fine. It seemed almost miraculous. I put Chica back in the coop and came back a while later.

It was then I understood what had happened. There was Chuckles smashing away at Chica with wings and beak. Chica was in the corner of the coop, down for the count. I threw open the door in anger and grabbed at Chuckles. She roared and fought me, but I drove her away and picked up Chica. She was practically limp, but after another night in the kitchen cage, she had again miraculously rallied. And there in the kitchen she stayed until it occurred to me that Chica didn't deserve this banishment.

I picked up Chica, went to the coop, and said, "Oh, Chuckles! Let's do some time sharing." I put Chica in the coop and went after Chuckles. It was a noisy catch with a lot of slamming about, angry cooing, and a cloud of feathers in the end, but I finally had Chuckles in my hands and brought her into the kitchen. She struggled, but I threw her into the cage. Chuckles looked about, took in her surroundings, and made a decision. She then busted out of the cage—just flew at the swinging wire door on the top and bashed it clean open and went right out, flying through the house. She had the brains of Squeaky, but not the good-natured soul. It took me a half hour to catch her and get her back in the cage, which I secured with a heavy river rock on top.

The next day, Chica and Lucky were billing. They had mated for life, and I savored a little satisfaction at that and went right to the kitchen and said, "Oh, Chuckles. I've got something to *tell* you!"

As the days passed, I began to resent Chuckles more and more. I punished myself for my blindness to what had been going on—for how many years? Had poor Chica, odd hen out, been in a pigeon hell that I had unwittingly devised? How long had I let that evil and jealous hen torment her? Finally, I decided to get rid of Chuckles. I couldn't put her back in the coop, and how long could anyone go on with a pigeon living in their kitchen for goodness' sake?

I put the cage in my truck and drove to the university. Getting her out of the cage was a battle royal. I finally got a good hold of her, but she fought me almost breaking free. To keep her in my hands, I needed to use so much strength that I thought I would crush her. I turned from the truck and tossed her out on the campus grounds. She alighted and then flew away. She was the strongest, most ferocious pigeon I had ever seen.

The next day Chica lay on the floor. There were ants on her, so I knew she was dead. The ants always know. I put her in the freezer with Squeaky.

Lucky was alone.

And he got old. And he couldn't fly. So I put some bricks on the floor of the coop for him to sit on. And there he sat through the burning summers, and the freezing nights of winter.

A JOKE—WEATHER—INCOMPATIBLE ROOMMATES—
SEVENTY-FIVE-WATT BULB—SPECIAL SEEDS—A
NIGHT OUT UNDER THE STARS—SIERRA POND

A man goes to a psychiatrist and says, "Doc, I've got a problem. My wife keeps a nanny goat in the bedroom. It's a pet. Now, I've got nothing personal against nanny goats, but this one happens to smell to high heaven!

The psychiatrist asks, "If that's the problem, why don't you just open the window?

"Are you crazy?" says the man, "And let out all of my pigeons?"

I never thought I'd be the man in that story.

How the summer heat might affect the pigeons never concerned me very much though I live in Arizona, and the temperature has risen as high as 123 degrees. I knew that Mourning doves sit on their eggs in the summer and rather than warm the eggs, the birds keep the eggs from frying by evaporative cooling. The adult bird simply begins to dry up in the sun, and the slowing evaporating bird cools the eggs. So I knew that doves could stand the heat.

In 2005 my dog Noodles died, and in July of 2007 I had a dream about her. I dreamed that I had left her on the shore of Lake Itasca in Minnesota, and in the dream I realized what I had done and went and found her and told her would never leave her again. In the dream, I gave up my airline ticket to drive Noodles back to Arizona. And so a few days later as I was walking back from the local saloon through the blazing 115-degree Arizona day it hit me: Like in the dream, I had abandoned Lucky in the coop, and Lucky was too old to take the heat anymore. I wrote in my journal that night,

July 8 2007: When I got home, I took Lucky inside in the air conditioning into my room in a nice cage ....How could I have left him outside any longer when it is 115 degrees? I scratch him on the head, and he likes it. God forgive me for the time I have wasted.

It was not to be as joyous a decision as I thought. I was soon to learn something about how Lucky viewed me and his world. This happened when I got it into my head to change the living arrangements. You see, I felt that the cage with its wire top gave Lucky an uncomfortable feeling of confinement. Outside, I had fastened a yard-square board atop a single post which I had embedded in a five-gallon can filled with cement. It was a bird feeder that I didn't use much, preferring instead to throw the seed on the ground for the Inca doves and other birds. If I brought it into my bedroom, Lucky could live on it. He couldn't fly, so if he didn't just fall off, it would be a perfect place for him.

I carried the heavy "table" in and tried it. Lucky fell off a couple of times, and I'd find him on the floor and put him back. But falling off was not the problem. The problem was that while in the past he tolerated me as a casual visitor to the coop, I had now become a permanent live-in. He used to allow me to pick him up and scratch him, and this agreeability I took to mean he liked me. I had mistaken toleration for affection. When I set him up to live in the bedroom, I learned that Lucky regarded me in an entirely different way. Now, I was not the occasional guest visiting briefly. Now, I was there to stay.

I would come into the bedroom, and Lucky would stiffen on the tabletop. He would growl and look up at me with the red eyes of a bull. He couldn't paw like a bull, but he did something I had never seen a pigeon do: he started batting, rapping his wing, where the bone met feather, onto the tabletop. The behavior was filled with aggression and perhaps even hatred. "Rappity rappity rap! " he was saying. "The creature visits itself upon me forever! The creature! Curses! Rappity rappity rap!"

I put Lucky back in the cage and put the cage in the kitchen where Chica and Chuckles had been. At least I wasn't in there with him. And so he stayed there until winter when he went back out in the coop.

Arizona winters are mild, but there are nights that freeze. On those nights, I always used to cover the coop with blankets so no icy draft would kill anybody. Now, Lucky was very old and sitting on the floor, so I ran an electrical wire out to the coop and plugged it to a metal desk lamp with a 60-watt bulb in it. I covered the lamp with tinfoil and put it just inches from where lucky would sleep at night. The blankets, of course, stayed. A little later, I swapped the bulb out for a 75-watter just to make things a little warmer. But it got to be a hassle, and now Lucky is back inside on the kitchen floor and has been for some time. And here he will stay.

His eyes have dried up and get stuck shut, but every day I pry the lids apart and put drugstore eye drops in, and the eyes seem to work fine even though they are now strangely almond-shaped instead of pigeon round. He bites me viciously when I put in the eye drops.

I go to the Sunflower Market and get specialty grains for him: flax seed, buckwheat groats, lentils, wheat berries, and mix them with milo and peas and corn and sunflower seeds, so Lucky eats like a king. But he bites me when I reach in to fill his tuna can with grain.

I take no offense and still try to do things to make Lucky's life a little more interesting. I used to take the cage out and set it on the coop and have a beer while Lucky had vacation outdoors under the sun. Once, however, I awoke one morning to find that I had left him outside all night on the coop, and I raced out in horror that the neighborhood cats might surely have gotten into the cage and killed him, but he was fine having spent nothing worse than a mild evening out under the stars. But I've quit putting the cage out back.

The other day, it was 112 degrees out, and it occurred to me that Lucky never got a bath, and pigeons love to bathe. I turned on the backyard hose with its nozzle in the little cement depression I had built and christened "Sierra Pond." The bloom was on the sage around the pond, and some of the purple flowers had fallen into the water. I got Lucky and set him in the pond. The water boiled beneath him, cool and bright in the burning Arizona sun. He floated, feet just touching the bottom, spinning in the water like a miniature armful of laundry. The almond eyes blinked. He spun slowly, wings extended over the shining water and the whirling purple blossoms.

HOW TO FLY AN AIRPLANE

It was late in the 1970s and I was readying to take a three-hundred-mile solo flight in a two-seat Cessna 150. The trip was part of my training as a private pilot. The flight school wanted me to fly from Houston to Austin and then on to Victoria and back to Houston, making three take-offs and three landings. I drove out to the airport that morning to start the trip by doing a preflight of the plane.

As I looked at the Cessna, a high-winged plane with tricycle landing gear (consisting of two main wheels and a nose wheel). I was struck as I often was by how truly small it was, and I felt a pang of self pity that was born of real fear. "You must be crazy," I told myself. "You're going to take off in that tiny tinfoil ship and rip along at a hundred miles an hour up in the air when you know darned well you're acrophobic." I steeled myself and started the preflight.

The preflight is the first step to any airplane trip. You have to check to see if anything is broken or otherwise wrong with the plane. You'd be crazy not to. I first walked around to the front of the plane and ran my fingers across the edges of the prop looking for dings. If there was any large notch there, I would cancel the flight until a certified mechanic had filed the area smooth. Popular theory said that if the prop broke while you were up in the sky, the imbalance could pull the engine out of the plane if you didn't throttle back immediately. With the engine gone, or yanked a foot to the side, the plane would acquire all the aerodynamic characteristics of a grand piano.

I pulled open the flap door to the engine compartment and stared in. All looked good to my uneducated eye. I saw four cylinders and eight spark plugs (spares you know) and I checked the oil. I had to wipe off the dip stick and test it again because during the cold night the oil had crept up and given an overfull reading. There was plenty of oil—and gas too, as I learned after climbing onto the wing, removing the cap, and looking into the tank. I would check the gauge later, of course.

I next checked the leading edges of the wings. Then I stuck a hollow metal pin into the bleed valve underneath one of the wings. The pin was fixed in the center of a thick, clear plastic cup into which a measure of blue fuel squirted from the gas tank. The blue color meant that the fuel was 100 octane gasoline. Reddish would mean 80 octane. I knew that if I needed gasoline, I would have to put 100 octane in the tank. You can only put the high on top of the low; you never pump 80 octane into a tank with 100 octane in it.

But I was not looking for the octane as much as I was for air bubbles that I didn't want in the gas lines. Bubbles collected at this bleed valve and the test alone would purge most of them. There were none I could see as I looked into the fluid, and I tossed the contents of the cup on the tarmac and put the cup in the glove compartment of the plane.

Next, I stepped over and grasped the wing tip and rocked the plane. The whole plane only weighed 1600 pounds and it moved easily but as one solid, collected piece. If the wing made any noises or didn't feel right, I would know it and have someone qualified look at it.

The pitot tube sticks out from under the wing like a little pointed faucet with a hole in the end. It gives you your airspeed. If there is a bug stuck in there, you'll get no airspeed reading. I knew this well, for once I had taken off with a mud dauber's nest clogging the hole and found I had no air speed reading on the control panel. I turned the plane around immediately and made a decidedly nose-low landing. How I didn't notice the malfunctioning airspeed indicator before I was in the air I can't really say.

There were many other spots to check: the brake lines, the tires, the trim tab connection in back, and my favorite, the tiny nut connecting the elevator to the cable. I hated the idea of having no elevator to control pitch and if that nut came loose or the cable broke, I would be in dire straits. An instructor had told me that that would be his first choice if he had to lose a control surface. He figured he could control pitch with the trim on the elevator or by lowering and raising the flaps. I thought he was crazy. No one could argue about a lost aileron (That would spell curtains.), but let the rudder break, I thought. I flew fine without it all the time.

The thing that keeps pilots alive perhaps more than anything else is the engineering that goes into the planes. The nuts and bolts and cables just don't break very often. They aren't Ace Hardware nuts and bolts and cables; they are the real thing, specially-engineered parts that are made to the highest industry standards.

In view of this attention to design and safety, it always amazed me to know that underneath the control panel in front of both seats were exposed chains that pulled the cables attached to the twin yokes. I am referring to chains in the bicycle chain sense of the word. The chains look exactly the same and they are right next to your pant legs and your shoestrings. For anyone who has ridden a bike without the chain guard and found himself or herself repeatedly parking the bike by falling over with their shoelaces caught fast in the chain, this will seem amazing. But it is true. Next time you get the chance, look under the control panel of any small plane and you'll see what I mean.

When the preflight was done, I unfastened the chains that held the wings and tail of the plane and let them fall to the tarmac next to their steel fittings. I got in the plane and put on the rather old fashioned seat belt and shoulder strap. I pulled out the pin that locked the yoke and put it in the glove compartment. Then I flipped the two red master switches that started the magnetos and avionics purring with that characteristic airplane sound that you hear nowhere else.

With my left hand, I grasped the key, looked around the plane, and shouted "Clear Prop!" I pushed the red mixture knob all the way in and then started the plane just like you do a car but adding the power with my right hand by pumping the black, cue ball-sized knob of the throttle. My toes were pushing good and hard on the upper part of the rudder pedals. The brakes were located there, the hinged top half of each pedal. The prop spun and the engine roared to life.

It was time for the run-up. I pushed the power to 1800 rpm and checked the oil pressure, voltage meter, and gas gauge. I then turned the key to the left, disabling one magneto. The rpm fell only slightly as expected. I did the same with the right magneto, turning the key to the right, and got the same effect. I left the key in the dual position so both mags would be on. Both were working fine.

When the plane was idling smoothly, I switched on the radio and turned it to the information frequency where I heard:

> *Hobby Airport information Charlie. Measured ceiling two two hundred. Visibility ten. Smoke. Haze. Temperature eight seven. Wind one eight zero at one one. Altimeter two niner niner zero. ILS runway two two in use. Landing and departing runways one eight right and one eight left, one seven and two two. All VFR and IFR departures contact Hobby ground one two seven point nine prior to taxi. Advise you have Charlie.*

I set the altimeter to 29.90 inches of mercury and switched the radio to the ground control frequency 127.9. I waited for a moment for everyone else to stop talking and said into the mike, "Hobby ground, Cessna 11452 at Fletcher's with Charlie. Negative transponder. Taxi to runway one eight right. Student pilot."

"Cessna 452 . Cleared to taxi. Hold short at runway one eight right," came the immediate reply.

"Roger" I said.

What I had told the ground control was that I had listened to Information Charlie ("Charlie" being airplane talk for the letter C) and was therefore informed about the current conditions of flight. Later, I might have to say that I had the latest information Delta (D for Delta). Fletcher's was the flight school and I told him that so he'd know where I was. I said, "Negative transponder" because the plane didn't have one of those expensive devices that detect radar and send back a powerful answering beam to the tower people so they know who and where you are. "Holding Short" meant I was to taxi up to the end of that runway but not drive onto it. "Roger" meant "I understand."

I had already phoned in a flight plan on the telephone and all I had to do at first was fly over to Austin and close the plan by phone.

My non-electric calculator and pencils and maps lay on the seat by my side. As my plane rumbled along the yellow-lined taxi way I saw a 737 coming in to land on runway 18 Right. Ground Control came back on with, "Cessna 452 hold short at Runway one eight right."

I picked up the black microphone, pressed the button and said, "Roger. I will hold short." The words "student pilot" had made the ground controller nervous. He didn't want me taxiing in front of a jet. But I didn't mind. I felt no pride about my abilities and felt more secure knowing that the controllers knew I was green. They'd pamper me some for the good of all and that was just fine with me.

Ground Control called back and said, Cessna 452 contact Tower point 7. I said "roger" and switched to 127.7 and said, "Hobby Tower, Cessna 11452 ready for take-off at runway one eight right." I clicked the mike again and added, "Student pilot."

There was static and then very clearly came, "Cessna 452 taxi into position and hold."

At small airports before I taxied onto the runway I often did more than just look out the window to check for approaching aircraft. I would often spin the whole plane in a circle as I looked out the windows and checked the whole sky for traffic.

I would do this by locking one of the brakes on the main wheels and pushing with just one toe on the top of the rudder pedal. If it was the left toe, the left main wheel would freeze and the rest of the plane would pivot to the left around it as I added the necessary power with the throttle in my right hand.

The rudder pedal also turns the nose wheel on a Cessna 150, so if I pushed the rudder pedal down too, it wouldn't hurt. The nose wheel is spring loaded so if you're sitting on the tarmac and want to test the rudders you can stomp on the pedals and only the rudder will move—not the nose wheel. The nose wheel spring just stretches if there's much resistance, and it doesn't turn. But if you are taxiing briskly or taking off, there's less resistance and the light pull of the cable attached to the spring becomes effective and you can steer with it alone. I always liked the fact that the plane would spin on a dime and it was fun to do a clearing turn at smaller airports.

Here at the big airport, things moved a bit faster. I could have spun the plane and no one would have complained, but instead, I just taxied the plane out onto the runway and stopped with my directional gyro reading 180. From Information Charlie, I knew the wind was coming from 180 degrees on the compass or south at eleven miles per hour, directly down the runway at me. The runway was named "one eight" because it ran south from this end and north from the other. The other end was named runway 36 because north is 360 degrees on the compass.

The tower waited a good bit before clearing me for take-off. There was a rearview mirror in the plane and a back window. I found myself looking in the mirror for aircraft. The wait, however, was really welcome and necessary because of the dangerous wake turbulence the 737 had left. It takes two or three minutes for it to dissipate.

When I heard, "Cessna 452 you're cleared for take-off," I said, "Roger" and pushed the black throttle all the way in; full power and nothing less is what you want with a take-off. The plane rolled down the runway and quickly picked up speed.

The take-off was fun as usual. It is a simple maneuver and if you keep the plane straight by steering with your feet, there's little that can go wrong. I held the U-shaped yoke with my left hand and gripped the throttle with my right. You never hold the yoke with both hands; the left hand flies the plane and the right works the throttle and other controls.

I looked at the airspeed indicator as it climbed across the numbers. When it hit sixty-five miles per hour, I lifted the nose with my left hand and the plane jumped into the air.

Now I had entered the airplane's other realm. I said that it was fun to make the plane spin in circles on the ground. It is. You can drive a plane on the ground (once you learn how) and you can do the same tricks perfectly every time. You can master the plane on the ground. In the air, it is a very different story. If you take a test with an FAA official who tells you to fly a certain course at 1200 feet, you can lose or gain 100 feet as you do it and still pass that test. You can always turn the plane on a dime when you are on the ground, but some days, you can't buy a good landing. The difference between the plane on the ground and the plane in the air is obvious very early on in your training.

Since I was climbing now, the nose was high and the instrument panel was all I could see. You can't see through the windshield of a climbing plane—well, you can, but the view is almost vertical and consists of only sky. The higher the nose, the steeper the climb, the slower the airspeed, and the less the visibility. It's like driving one of those old steam locomotives with no front window. Your view is completely blocked and if you want to see where you are going, you have to stick your head out the window.

I could never stand not being able to see and this time like most other times I lowered the nose until my climbing speed rose to 80 mph. I could see just barely over the control panel with the nose lower and I also took comfort in the extra wind over the wings to keep me aloft.

50

The plane was still climbing and with the nose raised there were other matters to consider. The plane is rigged aerodynamically for level flight. When the nose is high, however, the descending prop bites harder into the air than the ascending prop. This causes the plane to yaw to the left. The effect is magnified by the air that swirls from the prop. It washes over the fuselage and hits the left side of the rudder, increasing the yaw. You have to add some right rudder to counteract all this.

Even over an metropolitan area like Houston, the most appealing thing about flying an airplane is the view from the air—Once you leave the ground almost instantly you have a view that is almost Grand Canyonish is its beauty. You might think that people fly planes for the thrill of speed, but you cannot perceive that speed unless you are landing or for some other reason close to the ground where things are whipping past you. Almost always there is no sensation of forward movement—only a floating feeling as you fly a plane. I think most people fly more for the view.

I flew the plane around some radio towers I knew and made a one-eighty north, flying until I had the airport behind me. Then, I got on my heading for Austin.

The Astrodome passed beneath and I recalled that I had been this way before. I got lost on a trip to College Station and had to buzz a water tower as my mom, a WWII WASP pilot, always told me to do. The tower had "Municipality of Hempstead" painted on it, so I looked for Hempstead on the sectional map, found it, marveled at how far off course I was, and headed in to

College Station where the tower asked me to wag my wings so he knew which plane I was.

Nothing special happened on the way to Austin. The view was spectacular. The tower at Austin told me to climb to 2200 feet and I procrastinated a bit and he came back real soon and said, "Cessna 452, say your altitude."

"1800 feet," I admitted, embarrassed.

"Climb to 2200 feet!" he said sternly, and I complied.

The tower directed me around so I was coming in for a straight-in approach to runway 27 left, only I couldn't see 27 left, only 27 right with its big letters 27R. "Cessna 452, do you have the runway?"

"Negative," I answered, "I have only two seven right in view."

"You cannot see two seven Left?

"Negative. Only two seven right." I looked, but I couldn't see the other runway.

"Cessna 452, you are cleared to land on runway two seven right."

I felt relieved because I was approaching the airport so quickly and now had a place to land. I set the plane up to land with 30 degrees of flaps and was coming in low and slow over the runway when the tower shouted, "Cessna 452 Go around!"

"Holy cow," I thought, worried that I was in the way of an airliner or something. I said, "Roger," pushed the power to full, and climbed slowly away, carefully bringing the flaps up five and ten degrees at a time.

The tower cleared me to land on runway 27 again and had me make a one-eighty. Then I was flying back to try the same landing again.

It was a familiar routine for me to fly a downwind leg for a landing. The plane was moving at eighty miles an hour or so in a straight line parallel to the runway, which was a couple of hundred feet to the left. I would fly beyond the end of the runway and make another one-eighty to land on it.

The runway on my left moved by and when I came to its end, I pulled the throttle back to 1700 rpm and pulled the carburetor heat knob on. That's the first step to a landing. The carburetor heat knob lets unfiltered air rush around the hot manifold directly into the carburetor. It prevents ice from forming as the sucking carburetor cools the air that enters it at low rpms. You pull it out when you land and push it in along with the throttle when you take off.

With the rpm down to 1700, I reached down and gave the little black flaps tab a nudge and heard the electric buzzing sound of the flaps going down. I only put down about ten degrees.

When the flaps started down, the nose of the plane pitched up and I had to hold it down by pushing on the yoke. It took a little muscle to do that, so I reached for the trim wheel just under the throttle. I spun it up a little and it took that extra pitch out of the plane without my having to push on the yoke anymore. You are always adjusting that trim to take uncomfortable pressures off your yoke.

I made a 90-degree left turn called the "base leg" so that I could see the end of the runway through my left window and I added on more flaps, held the nose down and trimmed the pressure away. Then I turned to final approach, another 90-degree left turn that put the runway right in front of me. I added in the last of the flaps then and pulled the throttle out to nothing. The prop whirled in the wind with no real power as the engine merely idled. I was down to under seventy miles per hour.

You have to use your eyes when you land the plane. The runway is a long rectangle and its end is a straight line with a number on it. Neither that line, nor the number should move in the windscreen. They should stay right in the same place in the windscreen frame. If the runway appears to move up in the windscreen, you are too low and had better act to correct it. If the runway seems to fall in the windscreen, you are too high. You fly the plane so that the line at the end of the runway and the number simply grow bigger and wider in the same place in the windscreen. Soon they'll be very big indeed, and you'll be putting your wheels on them.

At the same time you watch your airspeed. The stalling speeds are marked there on the indicator and you cannot allow the plane to slow beyond the point of no return. One way to get killed is to stall the plane on the landing. I'm referring to stalling the wing, of course —not the engine. You don't really need the engine to land. You do need to keep the nose low so the plane doesn't stall.

The end of the runway spread out wider and wider in front of me and when I was about eight feet above the ground I gave a little tug on the yoke. The plane didn't flare, so I did it again and the plane stopped its descent for a moment and floated over the runway. Very gently I pulled the yoke back—and I kept pulling it back quarter inch by quarter inch until the stall warning horns were screaming. Nose high, I could see nothing in front of me except the control panel. I pushed in about five rpm of throttle just to spin the prop and keep the plane flying that much longer and then the main wheels behind me touched the runway and rolled rubbery without a squeak. I held the nose high until the yoke was back to its full stop and then the nose wheel came down and touched the pavement on its own. I could see in front of me again. A perfect landing. No one on earth could do it better. Still, I felt the sense of relief I always felt when the plane got safely back on the ground.

I switched to the ground control frequency and heard my instructions to exit via one of the left ramps. I saw an exit ramp and I slammed on both brakes and let the plane come to a shuddering near-stop. I put some extra weight on the left toe so the plane would turn that way as I gunned the throttle to move the slower, heavier plane around the axis of the left main wheel.

At the airport I made a phone call and closed my flight plan so they knew I had reached Austin safely and no one would start a search for me. It was hard to forget because there was a huge sign that said, "Did you Close Your Flight Plan?" Reminders like that are common at airports. Deer Valley Airport in Arizona has a good example of such a reminder. As you approach the runway, you see written in spray painted river stones the word: "Wheels."

I took off again and headed for Victoria. The flight was nearly south and I didn't bother to add in the positive degrees you add when you are flying west. The plane has a magnetic compass, but the sectional map shows true north, so you have to adjust with the "East is least, West is best" system to make up for that. That's a part of dead reckoning navigation, a little science that is quite impressive at times.

If you plot your course correctly and compute your heading (a course corrected for wind) you can time your passage over selected landmarks almost by the second. Let's say you have planned to power the plane at a certain rpm and a certain heading starting at a certain time. Your calculations on the sectional map indicate you will pass over a stock tank at 9:15 and 20 seconds. It's perfectly reasonable to make that forecast with your knowledge of where the wind is blowing and so on. But it is still an eerie feeling to find that the second hand of your wrist watch bears out the prediction just as you pass over that stock tank.

I said that a heading is a course corrected for wind. This means that if Victoria is directly south and a hundred miles away you can't just fly at 180 degrees at 100 miles per hour and expect to be there in an hour. You may have ten degrees of cross wind, in which case in that hour you will have flown ten miles off course and probably not even see the Victoria Airport. You have to add that factor to your course to get a heading that does what you want it to do.

There is no ignoring the winds aloft (or on the ground). The plane is imbedded in the air mass. If that air mass is moving at ten miles an hour to the west, the plane is doing that too. When you fly your heading and you are correcting for wind, the plane will fly sideways. This is called crabbing and it is the normal way to fly from one point to another. There's no other way. You must account for the wind to get anywhere.

One more point about being imbedded in the air mass: I have read newspaper articles that suggest that this plane or that plane crashed because the pilot turned away from the wind, lost airspeed and stalled. I have also heard people worry about the wind stopping and the plane losing its lift and falling from the sky. These things cannot happen. Again: the plane is imbedded in the air mass. If it's approaching the runway and the wind stops, the plane will simply increase its ground speed while maintaining its air speed.

When I got to Victoria I was met with a serious problem. It seemed that the airport was hosting some sort of twin-engine aircraft aficionado convention. The air was alive with planes. I looked at the approaching airport and there must have been twenty-five big planes on the upwind and downwind legs of the runway. I switched the radio to the local frequency and said, "Victoria Unicom, Cessna 452 entering downwind leg from forty-five for full stop on runway two two." By this I was telling everyone that I was coming into the downwind leg at a 45-degree angle and wanted to land and stop on the runway as opposed to making a touch and go.

I tried to get into the traffic, but the other planes were too fast. I gave up the effort almost at once and turned the plane around. I thought of trying to get back into the pattern, but when I flew back to do so, just one look at all those big, fast twin-engined monsters made me change my mind. I climbed to 3000 feet and went right over the top of the airport and looked down. There were a million of them. I suppose I could have got on the radio and begged everyone to get out of the way, but the whole situation was just too scary for me. I decided to fly back to Houston.

I put the plane on my predetermined heading and then realized I hadn't closed my flight plan. I freaked for a minute before I thought, "Heck, I'll just close that flight plan using the radio and open the new one the same way." I had to juggle some papers and things as I flew the plane and gave the people on the radio the figures they needed, but soon I was flying back to Houston's Hobby airport.

The trip back dragged and soon I wondered whether I was lost. None of the landmarks seemed to be on my sectional map. Finally, I saw a little kidney-shaped lake that matched the lake on the map exactly. I changed my heading by eyeballing the map, not even using my plastic protractor. A while later I saw familiar radio towers and I knew I was near home. I felt a kind of grateful lump in my throat over this. I knew that I was going to survive another flight.

I contacted Hobby Radar who passed me on to the tower. I came in to land on runway 22 and as I did I noticed that the runway was falling in my windscreen. I was high. I began a maneuver called a slip that I was pretty skilled at.

I put the left wing down and pushed on the opposite rudder. With the controls crossed this way, the plane flew banked and sideways toward the runway presenting a great deal of the door and fuselage to the wind. And with that drag on the plane, it just began to drop like a stone from the sky. Slipping is the best way to lose altitude fast, but you have to watch the airspeed and keep the nose down as you drop sideways toward the ground. You don't want to slip with any flaps on either.

The runway came up in the windscreen and I took out the slip by simply rolling the plane level and taking off the opposite rudder. Now I was making a good approach.

At the end of the runway, to my right, I saw a 727 waiting to take off. There was a slight crosswind that would like to push me in that direction, but I used my controls to counteract it. As I got closer, I could see the pilot of the 727 looking out the window at me. He had sunglasses on and a white shirt and tie. I'm sure I made him nervous, but I missed him by at least a hundred feet and landed full flaps on the runway. Another real nice touchdown. I left the flaps down because I thought the plane looked so cool that way, and when I asked to taxi to Fletcher's the ground controller asked if I was the plane that still had its flaps down. I said, "Affirmative." and raised them.

Back at the ground school, my instructor asked how I had done. "Fine, I said. "Er, there was a lot of traffic at Victoria."

"Was there?" he said smiling.

I never told him that I didn't make a landing there. I wanted credit for that flight.

YUCATAN TRAVEL LOG

ADRENALINE RUSH—SERIOUS BIRDERS—BINOCS—
PREP FOR THE TRIP—A FOLD-OVER BOOKLET—VIEW
FROM THE SKY—ELLIS ISLAND—JOHNNY BEEP BEEP—
WEIMARANER—TULUM—BIRDS AND RUINS—IGUANAS
—COBA—WE DRINK WITH THE WAITER—THATCHED
HUT BOY—ICKY FOOD—ICKY NUDE—TOPES—
YUCATAN TRIKE—BIOSPHERE PROJECT—ALONE IN THE
JUNGLE—A BOTTLE OF RUM—UXMAL—MOT MOTS—
ANCIENT BLOOD FEST—PROGRESSO—A SCARY
ASCENT—I BARF

When Greg's wife Dana went to visit her mother in Illinois, he gave me a call and asked me if I wanted to go bird watching for a week in Yucatan with him. Now, Greg has this traveling stuff down to a T. He studies the birds of, say, Peru for a year and then flies there and tries to identify as many of them as he can. Within the last few years he's been to England (twice), Malaysia, New Zealand, Australia, Africa, Peru, and a lot of other places. All for bird watching. He says, "I-I-I-I do it for the A-A DRENALINE rush!" He's the only person I know who watches birds for the adrenaline rush.

Believe me, he's serious about this bird watching stuff, though he says he's not—but then you look at him and Dana and they've both got on T-shirts with hawks on them. You look at Greg and he's wearing a baseball cap with a pair of summer tanagers on it and they've both got bird key chains and a vanity plate on their truck that reads COLIBRI, Spanish for hummingbird

(though I think Chupa Flores would have been a cooler name because it looks like it could be a person. "You seen Chupa around?" "Chupa Gonzales?" "Nah, Chupa Flores.")

Greg also used to have a really expensive pair of binoculars: 8X42 Elite roof prisms with about a six-foot close focus (so if you're tall, you can focus on any birds that land on your shoes), but someone stole them when he was in Africa and he had to get a replacement there and came up with a 200-buck pair of porros that he's kept ever since. They've got a nice wide field of view and a really bright image, but they just don't provide those extra yards of reach and the fineness of detail that my 300-dollar Swift Audubons do. Greg is oblivious to this because he hasn't been using really good binocs for a while and has forgotten what a big difference quality can make. The poor soul doesn't know what he's missing and walks through life unaware of his own plight rather like people who use Microsoft products. I've got to urge him to replace those stolen Elites with some good binocs.

Greg has been a friend of mine since the early eighties. He's in his sixties now and when I was just barely thirty or so I was happy to hang with this older but interesting character. He walks a little more stiffly now than he used to; he's had his feet operated on and I think his knees are bad, but he is a big stocky guy and still quite a bit stronger than I am. He fits into the category of guys that you try to wrestle with and then say to yourself, "Jesus, this is a strong son of a bitch and I'm going to take that into account in the future." Greg used to always get drunk and run up out of a

61

crowd and say, "Give me a kiss, you big silly!" And I'd fight him off but the next day I'd still have two thumb-sized bruises in the middle of both biceps where that fruitcake had grabbed me. He was taking after the others in the weird crowd of high school teachers. These guys think it's a hoot to kiss each other on the lips like Arabs and God you can just hardly stand it!

Anyway, Greg had already done this Yucatan trip and knew exactly where to go. I told him I would think about it and then I called him back and said I'd go.

"This isn't a vacation," Greg warned. "It's an adventure." He was trying to make sure I didn't think I was going to be lying on a beach in a flowered shirt swilling rum and chasing girls. Then he told me that the jungle would be hotter than blazes. Shoot, I thought, but by then I'd already committed and couldn't back out. I hate the heat. I thought it would be like Mexico City, where it's always comfortable. (Weather-wise; if you've ever lived there you know the city itself isn't comfortable at all.)

A couple of weeks later Greg came by with a ton of bird books and maps and we sat around and figured out the trip and took notes on the birds and drank beer and yucked it up.

Afterwards, I took Greg's list of all the birds he had seen in Yucatan on his last trip and looked each one up in some books he had lent me. I didn't study very hard because I'm lazy and because I knew Greg would be able to identify the birds for me when we got there.

I took his list, a nice fold-over booklet, removed the staples, and photocopied it. Then I whited out all his check marks and recopied it and made a screaming pink cover with the picture of a barred antshrike on it. I made an extra copy of the cover as the flyleaf. Then I stapled both books together with the big stapler at the office. Later, Greg was surprised to see that I had my own copy, but he wasn't impressed with this small effort on my part; he himself had painstakingly cut every plate out of a huge Mexican bird book and had all of them laminated and bound so he could look at them in the field without carting around the whole clumsy volume.

The plane ride to Yucatan was in an MD-80, flying rocket ship that goes straight up when it takes off. In a short time I could see out the window the usual red deserts of New Mexico and Texas and there were small towns in the middle of nowhere which looked like good retirement options. After we flew over El Paso, I saw a wild meandering river that coursed through a deep canyon. Over Mexico, from 29,000 feet I could see tremendous cliffs below, topped with green. I'd look down over the edge of these cliffs and it was a dizzying drop down to the rocky land below. When we were over the gulf, it was as if the plane were upside down; the view below looked just like clouds and sky. Only when we passed atolls did this illusion vanish to give way to shallow turquoise water over white sand.

We passed over the jungle of Yucatan and some of it was tall Tarzan-style jungle with trees that looked deciduous. The landing in Cancún was a straight-in approach that had the jungle only disappearing at the last moment before the plane flared and the wheels touched down for a real kisser of a landing.

Oh, what a fine little Ellis Island we encountered upon our arrival at Cancún Airport. There was a huge room with air conditioners that roared at the decibel level of a major earthquake, and creeps cutting in line, and bottlenecks, and screw-ups, and just forget it! I hate traveling. I honestly don't know why I go. It was dark before we saw the end of that line, but we finally got through. Then we picked up our bags and found a shuttle van to the rent-a-car place.

Our driver beeped his horn at everything he passed. "Beep! Beep!" He beeped at dogs on the sidewalks and at people in their houses and at parked cars. Sometimes he'd beep when there was nothing really beepable there at all. "Beep! Beep!" he went. He then explained that the shuttle trip would be three dollars each and Greg told him in Spanish "SSSSSure, but I just want to cccccheck in the office first because last time it was fffffree." How's that for "beep beep?" I thought.

Of course, the fee was immediately waived at Greg's words, but just for fun I took down the van's license plate number so I could report the driver and get him in trouble on the off chance that anyone around there cared about such petty larceny. It was good that I took down the number, because Greg left his goddamned binoculars in the van!

There was a lot of shouting in Spanish by Greg and me and the rent-a-car people threw Greg in a car and, armed with the license number, off they roared, headlights sweeping the road ahead as they raced to get the binoculars out of the van before Johnny Beep Beep found out what was what.

Twenty minutes later, Greg came back ashen of face and somewhat green about the gills—but he had the binoculars! "You numbskull!" I said. "This is Mexico and it's Sunday tomorrow and even on weekdays they sell the good binoculars along with the unspoiled beef. Good luck finding any!"

Greg confessed that in his gratefulness at having been spared a hideous fate he had also tipped Johnny Beep Beep. I sighed. I didn't even ask how much the tip was. I would have stiffed that creep with a smile. "A curse be on heads of thieves and liars!" I always say.

We rented a Chevy Monza and drove it through the tropical darkness to Puerto Morelos where we found an eleven-dollar-a-night flea bag called Hotel Amor. Its decor? Contemporary Flintstones.

The town was right on the sea and we went out in the quiet night to see the boats with their expensive outboards rocking peacefully in the water over the white sand. I walked out on a dock there and saw a huge Weimaraner dog there. I later found he had some affiliation with the hotel we were at because he would often come up and look through the windows of their cafe . He seemed kind of a tragic being looking in that way with his huge silver-gray, half human, Walt Disney head. The dogs of Yucatan do not seem to fit into the yellow Calcutta breed that so often inhabits the slummy cities and streets of the third world. Many are chocolate or black and white and in various sizes and shapes. You can fancy that some have a bit of Airedale in them, others a touch of springer spaniel.

Greg and I drank some beer at a couple of Hotel cafes. I had not had a drink on the plane so it was Miller time for me. In other words, I needed a belt. We tried to buy some rum at a grocery store, but there was an election the next day and they wouldn't sell us any.

The next morning, we drove to Tulum. As Greg always said, "The cool thing about bird watching in Yucatan is that all the good places are at the ruins. So you get to see the ruins and the birds at the same time."

Tulum was unusual in that it was a Mayan ruin on the sea. Spanish sailors would see these big stone buildings on the coast and just keep sailing on. Why mess with a big place like that where they might have an organized army and a lot of pyramids to sacrifice you on? The ruins were full of huge iguanas that you could approach rather closely before they scurried off to your relief (There was at first some question as to whether they might run up and bite you.). There were orange orioles and yellow-tailed orioles, and altamira orioles, and tropical kingbirds, all life listers for me.

We then went to Coba, another ruin down a long road through the jungle. Near it, we booked a room in a Club Med hotel. The hotel was on a lake loaded with alligators. There was a little dock with a thatched shelter at the end and on the shore a sign with a friendly-looking green alligator painted on it and the warning not to swim. The locals told me their standard story of the kid fishing out there in a boat who got his line hung up on the bottom. When he dove down to get his hook back, he found out too late that he'd snagged an 18-foot cocodrilo and it just ate him up.

Greg and I went to the ruins and did really well on birds. I got a ton of life listers. I remember one in particular. Greg and I decided to take a trail out into the jungle and we were way out there and I saw what I thought were great-tailed grackles and Greg said, "They're grooved-billed anis!" And I looked and they were! God it was hot in there, but worth it to see grooved-billed anis, which I have always wanted to see. They have the coolest bills—really big like a Brazil nut but black and grooved. Too cool. When we got back to the hotel there were a half dozen of them hanging around in the bushes by the parking lot.

The next day we went through those ruins again and went down another trail and spotted a black-headed trogan and masked tityras and a ton of other good birds. We wound up having a beer in an outside cafe by the lake. Montejo is the local brand of beer and it isn't too bad especially at the six pesos in these cafes compared to the 15 at the Club Med. There was a Mayan guy there who got into a big discussion with Greg about calendars and counting in the Mayan language. He said he had a bird book at home. He reminded me a lot of me: "I've got a BOOK on that at home!" He carried a little notebook like mine with him, and in it we wrote down the English names for birds he wanted to know about. Greg went and bought him a Montejo and even though he was the waiter, he sat down and drank it with us. From our table, I spotted a spectacularly colored purple gallinule walking on the shore and the Mayan guy knew the Spanish name, *gallineta*. Mayan mathematics is a bit dull and Greg and I got tired of making the effort. We bid him *adiós* and walked down the shore and saw a ruddy crake, which we both agreed was quite a good bird to see.

Otherwise the lake was surprisingly unbirdy. There were tropical cormorants and anhingas sitting on posts out there, but not even coots swam in the lake. Greg got out his scope and we drove to the far side of the lake and set it up. All we saw were the cormorants and anhingas. Neither bird produces a water repellent oil so that's why they were on the posts—to dry out in the sun. If they don't dry out a lot, their feathers get soaked clean through and the next time they get in the water they just sink to the bottom and drown. That's my theory anyway.

There was a neighborhood of thatched shacks on the lake shore and a kid came out and seemed to know what we were up to. He was full of enthusiasm in his plans to learn some English and he said he was a waiter at a restaurant. The way he talked made us know he felt he was really on the road up. He was happy he lived in such a low crime area in the jungle instead of in some big city. Somehow despite the dirt floors this little burg wasn't much different from what you might find in Illinois. But this kid's future was not as much a slam dunker as that of some kid in Illinois.

The hotel was a Club Med, but the restaurant had an awfully short menu. For breakfast you could get some scrambled eggs and some fruit and perhaps a side of beans, but there was no bacon or ham or sausage or pancakes or anything else. I, to this day, am still trying to figure out what the deal is with the food in Mexico. I hear people rave about it but, frankly, I cannot conceive of more poorly prepared and sloppily presented dishes than those which I typically encounter in Mexico. I feel that I am taking a real risk any time I eat anything in that country even when I'm in a fancy hotel restaurant. And if it is not utterly putrid it a the very least tastes borderline spoiled like it's been kept way too long. Why? Because it has! There! I said it.

Greg and I don't fight very much or get on each other's nerves too much, but there was one annoying thing I found out about him: he has no nudity taboo. He'd get out of the shower and hang around naked and I'd say, "Hey, what the hell are you doing?"

"What?" he'd answer mystified.

"Get the hell out of here, you nut. Put some clothes on."

"Hey, you'd never make it on the river," was his retort.

And he was right. The river crowd he was referring to often sit around and reminisce with joy about the time they group-mooned some poor Japanese tourists from their rafts.

"YYYou've got hhhang-ups, man." he accused.

"Maybe so, Dr. Full Monty Freud," I answered. "Maybe so. But in the meantime put some clothes on, you gruesome bastard. Christ, what a carcass!"

Greg got the message and began wearing clothes again.

The next day, after I warily picked at my breakfast, we drove through several Mayan towns on our way to Muyil, a birdy ruin.

Here's how the travel through these towns works. It's always exactly the same. You head through the jungle on a fairly respectable cement highway until you see a sign that says "Poblado Próximo" and another that says "Disminuya su Velocidad." Next, you see a 50 Km/

Hr sign and the crosswalk warning sign, "Cruce de Peatones." Then comes a warning of topes, killer speed bumps. You *have* to slow down for these and even the dogs know it because they lie in the street just beyond them knowing full well there will be plenty of time to laze up and stroll out of your way. There are topes all through the town and that's the cure for speeding.

An ever present sight is the Yucatan three wheeler, a human-powered device that is used everywhere for a broad range of transportation purposes. It's a normal-sized bike that has been turned into a tricycle. But it differs from other trikes in that the single wheel is in back and two bike wheels are installed in front on either side of a large square metal framework that can carry people or cargo. Often it is used as a taxi or as one might use the family sedan to take the whole clan down the road. Those with an entrepreneurial bent load it up with their taco equipment and have a portable stand. Many of them are equipped with fabric canopies to shade passengers from the sun. They are everywhere, and if I had the concession on them I'd be rich enough to buy one of those really expensive birding scopes and a lot of other nice stuff.

Muyil was hot and there was a slight mosquito problem. I found that the 6-12 I brought along wasn't a very good solution because it was a cream. You could rub it on your skin but it was a little to messy to go on your clothes. I got out my aerosol can and sprayed a different brand on my socks and shirt. Now, I was all set for the day. Around my waist was a fanny pack with the back pulled around to the front. In it I carried a bottle of water, a can of diet coke, a pack of Tums, a pencil, a notebook, a bird book, some mints, a tube of sunscreen, some old wrappers and other trash I hadn't cleaned out yet, and a 99-cent raincoat half as thick as a pack of cigarettes and only a little wider. I had an extra bandanna and a baseball cap stuck in there as well. I found that the bandanna was good in humid weather while a hat would often just turn your poor miserable head into a sopping, baking wick. My right pants pocket was stuffed with two-hundred dollars in pesos and in my wallet was another three-hundred and fifty. My camera, reading glasses, and binoculars hung smartly around my neck. Waddling around with all this gear made me feel very happy and professional and I would recommend this set-up to anyone. It is an excellent rig!

We saw a Golden-fronted Woodpecker, a Caribbean Elaenia, a Tropical Pewee, and a Yellow-throated Warbler at Muyil. The woodpecker is common in Yucatan and recognizably a woodpecker to the layman. Elaenias are real candy-colored yellow and black birds while the pewee is a drab gray flycatcher.

There was a sign on a path saying that it led to a lake and we asked some worker in the jungle how far it was. He said it was 900 meters and as hot as it was Greg balked at the idea of walking. The guy said we could drive down a dirt road to the lake if we liked. We just had to take the first left out on the highway. We took his advice and went to the lake in the car.

The lake was malachite green and very large— almost like a little inland sea. There was a gray wooden dock leading out into the water and a big red rowboat beached on the shore. A spotted sandpiper wobbled along the water's edge. I walked out on the dock and looked into the lake for alligators. I didn't see any. Greg was over reading a very new sign with Spanish and English captions. It sported full color maps of the lake and it told of the Biosphere Project that the lake was a part of. This was a real wildlife reserve and but for vantage points like this one, nobody was allowed in it. Greg said they didn't want poachers to screw things up. There were jaguars in the reserve and their coats bring a handsome price from unscrupulous boneheads who have enough bread to buy them.

We stayed a while at the lake and looked at rough-winged swallows which Greg said he thought were really Ridgeway rough-winged swallows, a different species. Then we drove the car out and headed for Felipe Carrillo, leaving my favorite reading glasses on the jungle road by the lake. Luckily, I had brought two other pairs.

Felipe Carrillo is a town near some jungle that is said to provide some of the best birding anywhere. It was kind of a disappointment. We drove thirty kilometers down the road recommended in the bird guide two days in a row and found the place pretty quiet with regard to birds. It was also quiet with regard to people: on the second day no one but us drove down that long jungle road except for a single truckload of workers. We did see the barred antshrike and the squirrel cuckoo there though and a number of other good birds.

We had a plan for each day on this trip. At each site we'd get up early and try to identify as many birds as we could. Then we'd drive a hundred miles and find a nice place or a dump and spend the hot part of the day filling out our bird lists and journals and swilling rum. Greg got a huge bottle of Bacardi the second day we were in Yucatan, and it was simply a task of coupling this bottle's contents with the necessary two to one ratio of coca cola each day until it was finished. Then, we'd buy another bottle. I never drink distilled liquor except on trips like this. And I would only buy rum because I somehow find that it is slightly harder to come to grief with this beverage than with others although all distilled beverages, including rum, require vigilance as you can quickly become excessively swizzled if you are careless. And then there is no telling what might happen.

We repeated our bird watching routine at Uxmal, the best ruins I have ever seen. The architecture there looks like that of an Ivy League college and is all in great condition. The Mot Mots were nesting in the rooms and since we were there really early we had the place to ourselves. You could not stay in some of the rooms in the ruins because the ammonia from cave swallow droppings was something like mustard gas. It drove you right out of there.

There was also an absolutely huge pyramid there. I asked Greg what he thought they used to do up there. I wanted to know whether they sacrificed people and threw them down the stairs Aztec-like and then cooked them up with chiles and tomatoes or what. Greg said they used to have some priests that would go up there and cut up their genitalia or maybe someone else's or their tongues and so on until they had a lot of blood flowing. Then they'd impress the crowd with the blood and win favor with the gods etc. He said no one was sure of all the details. I told him the details weren't necessary; I got the picture. It was the holy grail and the blood of Christ deal Mayan style. Nothing really changes.

The next day we headed into Progreso, a town right on the northern shore of Yucatan. This was a great place. We took a road on by some mangrove swamps and pulled off onto the side of the road where big equipment was tearing up the place and in the process giving us plenty of room to park away from traffic. There was a tri-colored heron out there and when I scanned the shore near us I said, "Hey! A Wilson's plover!" Greg was happy to see that bird. I know he'd seen it before down at my family's beach house, but he had forgotten. "Do you see that one down at the beach?" he asked. "Sure," I said.

You don't run across a Wilson's plover very often and what's more, the bird falls into the same category as even much more common birds. That category is the anytime-is-a-good-time-to-see category. I invented this category myself. Anytime is a good time to see a yellow-headed blackbird, for instance. Certain birds just fall into this category even if they're common. The long-billed dowitcher falls into it. So does the greater yellowlegs. It's all subjective, of course. I like shorebirds such as the Wilson's plover. I like the way shorebirds wade around in the water and hang out on the beach. I get a vicarious pleasure from watching them root around in the water. So naturally I put more of them into this category than others might. Your tastes may vary. I've heard of people who have even put yellow-rumped warblers into this category.

After we saw the Wilson's plover we went down the road and saw about 1000 flamingos. When they fly, their stretched-out necks make them measure about ten feet from beak to tail. I was quite surprised at them and said, "Greg, the greater flamingo is one long drink of water."

Progreso hosted us with rather run-down quarters that were nonetheless on the beach. There were green cement walls all along the beach and cafes and bars and live music all down the strip. When Mexicans have vacation, this is where they come. I noted to Greg that a kid living is this place would likely think he lived in the greatest place on earth. He'd be wrong, of course, but he'd think it all right.

Only a half mile down the strip was a huge cement pier stretching out to the deep water of the gulf. Lines of big trucks rode out onto it to the multi-storied customs building far at the end. We were told that the pier was built so that big luxury liners could berth right up close and bring business to town. Someone miscalculated, however, because the water at the end of the pier was not deep enough for the really big liners to lie up close, so now they all ignored Progreso.

We went out into the night and found an amusement park with Ferris wheels and other rides. We just looked. We didn't ride. Then we hit one of the bars on the beach and guzzled some brandy and called it a day. Progreso was a very interesting town and I'm sorry to say I did not take a single picture there.

We had another Club Med hotel left on our agenda and that was the one at Chichen Itza. I have always wanted to see that spectacular pyramid there and so in the morning we got up early as usual and went over there.

I decided to climb the pyramid, but when I'd gone up about twenty steps I remembered how acrophobic I was. I knew the climb was scary, and when I looked up, it seemed like a climb to the moon. I was afraid to look down. Then I steeled myself and started heading up again on all fours. Finally I saw the line that marked the end of the last step and I pulled myself over the top. I was woozy just looking down. God, I was up high. The stones were all wet and slippery with dew and the view below was obscured with ground fog. I hated it up there, but I took a few foggy pictures just to show how hairy it was. Being up there was like something out of a nightmare because I still needed to go down those 45-degree steps each a foot high and 360 of them at that (one for each day in the Mayan calendar). You slip on these steps and you go clear to the bottom. Guaranteed.

Soon there were more people at the top. You'd step out of the room on top and bump into someone else coming around the corner. No rails. Nothing. I marveled at kids dancing clean up the steps to the top and backpackers just hiking up like it was nothing. Was I crazy, or was this not a damned dangerous climb? I looked and saw a hiker just trot down the stairs from the top three hundred and sixty feet to the bottom. Some French guy saw that I was acrophobic and motioned in sign language that he'd go down with me, but I finally crept over the edge myself. There was a rope in the middle and I hung on to it until I was ten steps from the bottom. Then I turned and trotted down.

Greg was waiting there. He said the sign said not to go up if you were over sixty or acrophobic or under eight years old. I talked to some Mexican guys and they said that tourists fell all the time. Often, they said, the people's legs would get torn up. Often they died on the spot. Just two weeks before, a seven-year-old had fallen to his death.

The best bird watching in Chichen Itza was at the expensive hotel we stayed at. They had a huge garden full of trees and there were chachalacas and even acaris in there. A chachalaca is a big long brownish bird and an acari is best described as a small toucan. Greg and I got some patio chairs and put them out there and mixed some drinks and just sat out there knocking off the occasional life lister.

All trips must end and frankly I get tired of hanging around so long. I get anxious to be back to my computer and TV and my dog. We took the car back to where we started, Puerto Morelos, and got a better hotel room than we had there the first night. We ate at the restaurant there and I was a fool and ate the beef, which I always mistrust and in the middle of the night I became nauseous. I got up and tried unsuccessfully not to wake Greg as I headed for the bathroom and shouted the paisley hurrah.

I was nauseous for a week and a half even after getting back to Arizona and the twelve-pack of diet coke a day that I poured into my stomach was comforting but not a cure.

The bird count at the end of the trip for me was 91 species 65 of which I had never seen before.

LURE LORE

The Fred Arbogast Company's Jitterbug is the finest top water fishing lure ever produced—bar none. I know this for a fact and so I was not surprised when Field and Stream featured it as a milestone in its 90-year anniversary issue. The Jitterbug is three inches long and in the shape of a stretched-out egg. It has a large paddling lip in the front and two large treble hooks hanging underneath. That's all there is to it, and nothing you can fish with on the surface can beat it for catching largemouth bass. Yes, I said nothing, and if someone has a different opinion, I'm not even going to argue. I know too much.

I learned about the Jitterbug rather early in life. The family was about to embark upon one of many summer stays at Lake Itasca in Minnesota. My father had a teaching job at the biology station for the University of

Minnesota and before we left on that first trip I asked him if I might get a decent fishing pole since I had never had one and he said, "Yes, Tommy, I think you deserve a good fishing pole."

The result was that my brothers and I soon were equipped with the absolutely cheapest rigs in the store. There wasn't much money when I was a kid—but those rigs turned out to be the best possible choice; we got fiberglass rods with Zebco 202 reels, and second only to my praise of the Jitterbug is my praise for Zebco closed-faced spinning reels. You can ask my friend Jan if you don't believe me. He said just the other day, "You know, I went ahead like a fool and bought a Johnson reel and I'll never be so dumb as to stray from Zebco again."

That pretty much proves my point. But I digress. I was going to say that my lure lore learnin' all started on our first summer in Minnesota. We'd fished before, of course—shoot, from Maine to Alaska—babies we were really—nearly freezing to death every night on 80-day camping trips in the early 1950s. But as for fishing, we were lucky to be outfitted with anything much better than a stick, ten feet of kite string and a bent nail. Now, however, we had two-dollar Zebco 202's and Field and Stream Magazines and a tackle box full of dreams.

At this early stage, I didn't know a thing about lures and I didn't really see how they could work. I figured you'd need some kind of bait on the lure just to make the fish interested. I held up one of the few lures we owned, a red and white Bass-Oreno and thought, "Well, I could hang a chunk of Swiss cheese on that hook and some hot-dog meat on the other and it should just about do it." I had a long long way to go.

On that first summer trip to Minnesota we spent the long days on the highway looking at the ads in Field and Stream—and how those magazines set us to dreaming about the fish we would catch! There was no end to the fascination that the fishing lure ads held for us and we would read and then stare misty-eyed out the car windows, read and stare again. There were Hellbender lures, and Super Sonics, and River Runts, and Pikies, and Sputterbugs, and Silver Minnows, and Dardevils, and Cisco Kid Divers. The brands seemed endless.

Soon however, it came to our attention that the tackle box did not contain all the proper lures in it. In fact, it had very few at all. We sought to remedy this with a few purchases in the tackle stores along the road to Itasca.

The first fish I caught on a lure was on this trip. I caught it in Fort Pierre, South Dakota. I still have the lure and I still have the jaws of the fish I caught with it. The lure was a Canadian Jig Fly. A guy at the cafe in Ft. Pierre gave it to us. He heard us talking about fishing and came over with the jig fly and said, "Oh, use this! This is a great lure." And he just up and gave us the rather expensive jig fly for nothing. I wish I could thank him someday and let him know how his act of kindness paid off exactly as he dreamed it might. The fish was a walleyed pike, a kind of large, toothy perch. Here's the lure and the upper jaw:

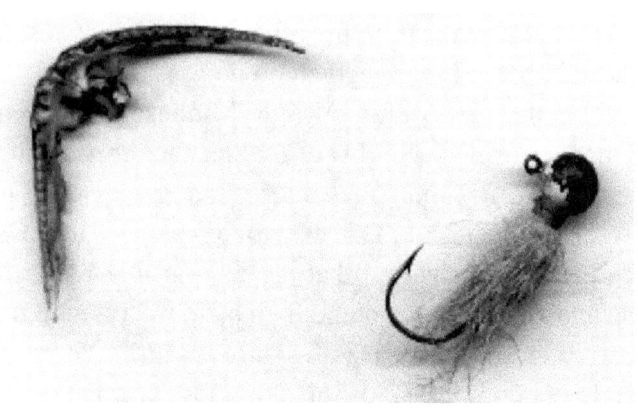

I caught the walleye at night in the tailrace waters below Oahe Dam. Steve caught two mooneyes there, which are large, eerie-looking minnows with tremendous owl-like yellow eyes. Oh, they were cool. I put the walleye up in the woods when we got to Minnesota and by the time summer was over, the deer flies had left nothing but bones and I brought back his jaws.

I keep those jaws along with the Canadian Jig Fly in my "Prized Possession Box." This is a box named by my friend Jan when we were kids. We found two identical jewelry boxes while we were raiding trash cans in Tempe and we vowed to put items like this in the boxes. This vow actually took and we each have a picture of the other in the boxes as well as a lot of other fabulous treasures and pieces of our lives. It was sort of a blood brother thing.

I have a chunk of Jan's original pigeon coop. It's the only piece that exists and he wants it, but it's mine. I have the first wood shaving I made in wood shop and my milk teeth and a chunk of something Jan and I found in a canal and couldn't identify and so I kept it. He has the other half of it in his box and we still don't know what the hell it is. In seventh grade, the pencil sharpener broke and carved spirals in my pencil and I kept that too. I've got a Lucky Lager bottle cap with a bullet hole shot through it and the tip of the garden hose we brought from Louisville to Tempe in 1959 and a firecracker I saved from a long trip through Mexico in 1963 and a 20-centavo piece that Jan and I put on the railroad tracks to get flattened. When I looked inside the old family piano a couple of years ago, I found an old guitar pick that I recognized from 1966 or so and I put it in the box too. I also have more recent items like the beer bottle opener I used when I lived in Mexico City and a piece of the shirt I wore when I first soloed an airplane and a slip of paper that reads "John Lennon Died Today." I was sure to write that note so I could put it into the box with the following one:

Jan's got basically the same stuff in his prized possession box. We don't obsess with these things at all, but if we deem an object worthy, it goes into the box.

Another kind of box that Jan and Steve and I keep are our old tackle boxes. They are full of lures that evoke a million memories and none of us would ever fish with these lures again and risk losing them on some snag or in the jaws of an especially strong fish. These lures are retired.

But back to the trip. The first thing we did when we arrived at our assigned cabin on Lake Itasca was to go down to the lake and try out Steve's new Poppin' Frog that he'd bought along the road. It was a weedless rubber lure with which we were all most intimately acquainted because it was featured in the most spectacular ads in Field and Stream. The ads showed the green, frog-like popper dancing between lily pads just over the jaws of a tremendous largemouth bass that would in seconds inhale it. He still has the Poppin' Frog.

It was night and raining off the little docks on the water and Steve started tossing that lure out and popping it with quick jerks of the pole and rock bass were coming up and hitting it every time he threw it out. He couldn't hook any of them because it was a weedless lure and as such was also fishless.

The double hooks were underneath the frog's body and they pointed upwards resting flat against the rubber. The idea was that when the fish bit down, it would squeeze the rubber out of the way and expose the hooks. Only it never happened that way. The "Poppin' Frog," aptly named, would just "pop" out of the fish's mouth. Steve flipped the hooks around so they faced down with the points in harm's way and started catching rock bass with every other cast. He was astonished to see me do the same with my simple cork popper that was not half as fancy or well advertised. (Oh, how I wish I had time to describe the rock bass and to tell how it had blazing ruby red eyes and hamburger grill flanks and spines that would draw your blood and how it would hit any lure and how it was a fisherman's cosmic last resort, and how we loved and hated it for the finny wonder and the trash fish that it was!)

And so it was that we began to learn about lures.

As I said, the Jitterbug is the finest top water lure ever invented, but we used others such as my cork popper, Steve's Poppin' Frog, my Ding Bat and Steve's Whopper Stopper Popper. Let me tell you about these top water lures.

If the Ding Bat was something of an antique back then, it's surely a collector's item today—and yes, I still have it. It is the size and shape of a prickly pear fruit with the front gouged out. It is also one of those lures with tasteful and elegant cosmetic appointments. It has glass eyes with black inlaid pupils, the traditional violin finish of a good guitar, and two tufts of bristly hair sticking out the back. The Ding Bat, like most large surface plugs came equipped with two large treble hooks. I used to drag that Ding Bat through the reeds on the far side of the lake and the bass would just come up and swallow it.

Steve's Whopper Stopper Popper was similar but more utilitarian and had black chevrons along its yellow side. He did well with it but he also had a yellow Jitterbug that would simply massacre the bass—just massacre them. Once he hooked a bass so big that the Jitterbug looked like a peanut in its mouth. The bass broke the line but shook the lure that floated to the surface of the lake where Steve later found it.

One summer, James Underhill, the father of my friend Bill Underhill, took me and some older guy out night fishing in a rowboat on Long Lake. I started using a Hula Popper by the Fred Arbogast Company, makers of the Jitterbug. The Hula Popper has a little rubber skirt attached to it and I guess one day when Fred Arbogast looked at the skirt some bell rang in his head and he thought it looked like a hula skirt and he went crazy and put a Hawaiian theme in his products. Thus, you could buy a Hawaiian Wiggler, a Hawaiian Spoon, a Hula Popper, a Hula Dancer ("Small but Mighty!" the ad went.) and so on. The Hawaiian theme really seems silly to me.

Anyway, the Hula Popper was (and is) in my opinion pretty worthless. I caught some rock bass on it, but then I switched to Steve's yellow Jitterbug, which I had borrowed, and soon had hooked a huge largemouth bass. I fought him until he was at the side of the boat, but then I foolishly tried to lift him aboard and the hooks were torn out of his mouth by his out-of-water weight. The bass crashed back into the lake and the Jitterbug whipped into the air at the end of the line.

"What did you do that for?" Asked Jim Underhill. "I was going to grab him by the lower jaw."

When I got home I was still crushed by the incident and the next day Bill Underhill came up and said, "Hey, my dad says you're a lousy fisherman."

"Oh, yeah? Nice of you to pass that on."

"Yeah," Bill laughed. "He says you horse 'em in, and that that bass must have weighed six pounds!"

There are a lot of other great lures and among the best is the Lazy Ike. It's a sinking plug shaped kind of like a humpbacked worm or something. It comes with two really high-quality treble hooks that are sticky sharp. Steve got the perch finish model because he thought it would look like a yellow perch so common in Lake Itasca. It was dark green with orangish-yellow triangles along its length. And man was it a killer. We used to troll with it around a certain point on the lake and he would catch more walleyes than anyone could believe on that thing.

Walleyes, by the way, are one of the most interesting fish I know and people go mad for them the way people go mad for bass. Walleyes, unlike northern pike, can see quite well at night and when the sun goes down, they move up from deeper water and go out on sandy flats to feed. We used to take a canoe or rowboat down to the swimming beach at night and land on the floating dock out there. Then we'd stand on the dock and cast bright spinners, which walleyes love, to the sandy shore and reel them back toward us. If the walleyes were there, they'd start hitting like mad.

In Arizona there are walleyes in Canyon Lake and if you take a boat and go way in there and camp in any of the few places you can find to do so, you'll likely be awakened at night by eerie lights and a dark shape on the water and a swish swish sound. It's just the walleye fishermen who use their electric motors and lights as they cast spinners out for Arizona walleyes.

Let me tell you something about spinners. A spinner is basically a wire threaded through some narrow body with a feathered treble hook at the end and a shiny blade in front. When you draw it through the water, the blade spins making a lot of flash and vibration. There are expensive brand name spinners like the Rooster Tail, the Mepps Fury and so on, but it was always my custom and necessity to buy the cheap imitations. They worked about as well, but the materials were shoddier is all. Once in Mexico, I hooked a spinner on a rock and gave it a tug and the spinner flew off like a bullet and hit me in the hand. The cheap hooks broke off in my hand and I just pulled them out because they hadn't gone in deeper than the barb. The name brand lures had better hooks all right. I remember when my friend Bobby Valdés hooked a South Bend Super Duper on the living room carpet and gave it a tug that set it flying into his knee. The doctor had a heck of a time trying to come up with a pair of wire cutters that would break the hooks. Before the doctor even tried, Bobby told him, "You'll never break those Super Duper hooks." But eventually the doctor prevailed.

I only really got hooked once good. I was alone in Mexico for a couple of weeks and was walking back to the beach house with my tackle box. Unbeknownst to me was the wisp of line that stuck out of the closed tackle box lid. It had a hook on the end of it and as I swung the tackle box rhythmically at my side that hook caught me in the back of the calf and just buried itself there. I took a pair of pliers and pushed it all the way through so I could cut the barb off with wire cutters. Strangely, it still wouldn't come out. Then I realized that the shank also had little barbs on it but they pointed in the opposite direction of the now absent main barb, so I had to cut the eye off the hook and pull it out backwards. Worked good—and it didn't hurt too much either. But I wanted to finish talking about spinners and then move on to jigs.

Walleyes and trout like spinners and so do crappies. And most everything loves a jig like the Canadian Jig Fly. A jig is basically a hook with feathers or hair on the end and a heavy round weight in the front. The eye of the hook, though, is bent up at a right angle to the shank, so you can make the lure hop as you lift the rod tip. Fish are said to perceive the jig as a minnow and this is what makes it so effective against minnow-eating fish like crappies and walleyes. A jig with a rubber body and a split tail is called a beetle because it resembles a beetle grub. I still have Bill Underhill's Super Beetle at home.

There are also deep diving plugs and they are more popular in rocky Arizona reservoirs than in natural Minnesota lakes. Diving plugs are floating lures that are pulled underwater by the huge lip in front. The faster you reel or troll, the deeper they go and the more they wiggle. I've always been fond of them even though they get hung up down there and tend not to go straight if the lip is only slightly bent and they start veering to the right or left, and I hate that. So I often troll deep by letting out more line with a flashy spoon on the end. I like spoons.

The Arbogast Company manufactured a deep diver called the Arbogaster and I bought one, but gosh it was a clunky thing with clunky action and if I were a fish and saw something that looked like that coming at me I'd get the hell out of the way fast. I feel the same way about Bomber Lures' "Bomber." The thing looks like a cartoon bomb. It's intentionally made to look like that with the big fins. The fins are the diving lip and pull the lure underwater when it is retrieved. When the Bomber hits the bottom, it scuttles along and is said to be perceived as a crawdad by the bass. I don't like them. I just think they're cheap and dumb and have bad Karma and so I never use them. They're so popular, however, that I thought they had to be mentioned. And I have quite a few of them at home.

Another way to get your line deep down is to use a down-rigger system. This involves specialized equipment that is installed on the back of the boat. There's a huge, very heavy streamlined fish-shaped chunk of lead that is hung from a cable that comes out of a little wheel off the stern. This lead fish weighs a ton and you let your fishing line out about fifty feet so it's trailing behind the boat and then hook your line to the lead fish. It's so heavy that the cable attached to it doesn't pay out when you lower it down sixty feet or so. The cable hangs straight down and the heavy lead fish is hanging directly beneath the stern with your line clipped to it and your line is still trailing out fifty feet astern with a lure or bait on it. The lead fish keeps your lure super deep. When a big lake trout or other dweller of the depths takes your hook, your line pops off the heavy lead down-rigger and you play him just as you normally would—only he's way down there and your job is to play him to the surface and net him.

I must confess now that I've never used a down-rigger, but I've seen the results. In 1987 Steve and I took another trip to Fort Pierre and fished the tailrace waters trying to relive the experience of so many years past. We got skunked, but when we went to the tackle shop some guys walked in with these absolutely gigantic salmon that they had caught using down-riggers. It seemed a little strange to see this kind of fish where we were—in the middle of the continent on the Great Plains—but we were told that the waters above the dam ran deep and the salmon fishing on Lake Oahe was some of the best in the world.

I said that the Arbogaster lure had clunky action -so does the Heddon Flatfish (Gad what a lure. Don't get me started.). But it is not really how you feel about the lure's movement so much as it is the fish's opinion that really counts. The Mirrorlure is an excellent example. It is a medium-depth sinking plug that is jointed in the middle. That is, it runs rather shallow when you retrieve it and there are two halves to the lure that are joined by a couple of connected eye rings in the middle. This jointed feature makes the lure wiggle just like a minnow. I'm telling you it looks EXACTLY like a minnow to the human eye. The fish, however, won't touch it with a freaking barge pole. I've never even gotten a strike on one.

What I have done well with are spoons. A few years ago the spoon bug bit me and I sent away for every kind I could buy. It cost quite a bit of money, but I've got a great collection.

The standard and most famous of spoons is the Dardevil and the classic red and white color is the only kind to buy. To get a feeling for the geist of this lure, here's one way to look upon it, and if you know anything about anything you'll get the idea: the red and white Dardevil is to spoons what the sunburst Fender Stratocaster is to electric guitars. That just about says it all.

The red and white Dardevil is used in the wholesale butchery of northern pike. For some reason, northern pike are just suckers for these lures. No one knows why, but they just never learn to stay away from the things.

Now, northerns, as we call them, are almost totally blind at night so you've got to use your spoon in the day. You will also need a swivel clip to attach to the lure or else the wobbling spoon will twist your line and make a tangled mess of it. You'd also best use a steel leader attached to the spoon or the pike will bite through the line and get away. (Actually the sierra mackerel is the undisputed king of line biters. Oh, I could tell you stories!) A northern pike will also bite you so you should keep your hands out of his mouth— although one look at a pike and only an imbecile would need the warning; the fish has more teeth than a dental supply house. (Walleyes will also bite you and come to think of it, so will English sparrows. Have you ever caught one? Ouch!")

In the same vein as lures are the little rigs and conventions you use to catch fish. There are two such that are absolutely essential for fishing and they are the improved clinch knot and the egg sinker rig. Anyone who can't tie an improved clinch knot in his or her sleep simply can't fish. Here's how to tie one:

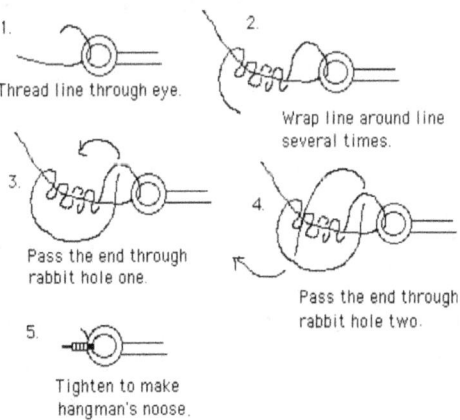

1. Thread line through eye.

2. Wrap line around line several times.

3. Pass the end through rabbit hole one.

4. Pass the end through rabbit hole two.

5. Tighten to make hangman's noose.

The egg sinker rig sure is useful. Here's what you do: take a heavy egg sinker which looks just like one of those small chocolate Easter eggs and thread your line through the hole that goes through it from end to end.

Next, tie a hook on the line and put about a foot and a half of line between the hook and the egg sinker. Then squeeze on a split shot between the hook and the egg sinker. The split shot will keep the egg sinker from sliding down to the hook.

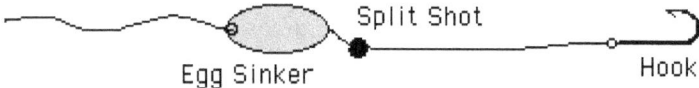

Now, when a fish bites, he will only feel the weight of the little split shot and not the egg sinker. A swivel clip positioned where the split shot is works even better because it's so light the fish will never notice it.

As the fish moves off with the bait, the line will pay through the hole in the egg sinker. You'll be wise to the fish because you've been waiting to see the line move. When you think the time is right you spike him good and hard.

Mounting your pole in the ground and putting a little fishing bell on the tip is a lot of fun with this rig. When the fish pulls, the bell rings and you can put down your beer and haul him in. You can also reach over and give a little shake to the fishing pole next to yours and watch your buddy explode into action. It's hilarious. If your friend doesn't have a bell, you can always holler, "You've got one!" How they scramble at this and how we laugh ourselves silly afterwards!

Anyway the egg sinker rig is the rig my friend Jan and I always use when we go to Mexico. There's a group that fishes out on the beach and it got to the point that when they saw us coming, they'd say "Oh, here come those guys that always put us to shame."

It was their own fault. You have to use at least common sense when you fish and these people never had any. They'd fish with their bait two feet from shore with the waves knocking it around. Jan I and would just sling those egg sinker rigs out there—I mean out there. Then we'd take in all the slack and watch for any movement. When we saw any we'd say, "Steady... steady... hold. ... Goose him!" And then set the hook. We'd always catch some yellow finned croakers or other nice fish.

Once we caught a couple of sand sharks and picked them up by the tail and tossed them back in. Then we saw one of these knuckleheads with a sting ray and he was following our example picking it up. We shouted, "Hey, don't pick that thing up! It'll sting you." to which the guy replied, "A stingray's got a pointed tail." The sting ray twisted itself up and stabbed its stinger in the guy's wrist. The stinger hit an artery and the guy held up his arm, watched the rhythmic pulse of squirting blood for a second or two and then his eyes rolled back in his skull and he collapsed on the sand

I remember Jan's eyes also rolling in an "Oooooh shit," kind of way because we both thought the poison had gone to the guy's heart or brain and had killed him or something. Fact was; the guy couldn't stand the sight of his own blood and just keeled over when he saw it. (Ain't nothing wrong with that!) But he had still been stung by a sting ray and no matter what we did, his friends and he would not take any of our advice about treating the wound. Sting ray venom is heat labile and hot water is the preferred treatment because when the poison gets hot, it breaks down and the pain stops in a few hours.

They took him back to their house, put ice on the wound and said, "Just go to sleep, Johnny." Yeah, we thought, so you can't see if the poison is having any awful effect on Johnny Boy. It was a moot point, though, because you can't sleep with a sting ray sting. Finally, they had to take him to the hospital, but they waited against our advice and let him suffer all night. The dumb dumbs.

There is another thing I'd like to point out about fishing lures. It's a new kind of hobby that I invented myself. It is lure hunting.

Whenever the fishing is bad, it is often possible to make up for it by going on a lure hunt. It's fascinating, fun, and profitable. In fact, there was a point where I just stopped buying lures. I didn't have to because I could always find them for nothing.

Anglers usually lose their lures in brush or trees along the shore or by snagging some obstruction underwater. Why a fisherman who snags the shore with a six-dollar plug doesn't get out of the boat and retrieve it is beyond me. But I've found some high-priced plugs hanging in plain sight.

Surprisingly, lures hooked on the bottom are the best for the lure hunter.There are two scientific laws that account for this: iron rusts and lures float. Most deep diving and medium-running plugs are floaters. When their hooks corrode away, they are freed from their underwater snags and are washed up on shore. A productive strand of beach, then, doesn't have to be right next to a fishy cove or point where anglers can be seen daily. I've found lots of plugs on lonely, rather fishless beaches on lakes in Minnesota and Arizona.

Diving for lures with a mask and snorkel is also a lot of fun and it can give you a better perspective of the area to be fished. Around half submerged brush along with snagged lures, I used to find hidden sunfish nests. I usually reached down and scratched the gravel there with a finger until the sunnie came and batted my hand. If I wanted to catch a sunfish, I knew where to go, though it seems dirty pool to catch them on their nests. They'll pick up anything that lands on the nest and carry it away.

In Saguaro Lake, I was once snorkeling ten feet deep exploring a very rocky, slanting bottom for lures. I followed a line to a large and handsome red and white brass spoon. After I freed it, I swam a little farther out and found that the rocks disappeared giving way to a flat underwater bar of sand and gravel. No one on shore had even thought of bottom fishing. It seemed that with all those rocks, the bait would simply fall between the cracks out of sight.

When I got out of the water, I made a rig with a split shot, egg sinker, and treble hook and baited it with Catfish Charlie stink bait. Then, I tossed it out over the rocks to my underwater sand bar. In only a couple of minutes a nice channel cat tapped at my line. I hooked him and brought him in. Whenever I go back to this area, I find that this unfished bar is always good for a cat.

What to do with the lures? I just keep them in boxes now, but I used to be more active. Many of the plugs I used to find needed new hooks. A good number of them, after all, had rusted themselves free from underwater snags. There was no problem changing the hooks on spoons, spinners, and plugs. Spinner baits, however, were a different story. I once was following my friend Jan, who was hunting lures with me at Roosevelt Lake when the water had fallen several feet. I came to a once submerged dead tree from which hung a beautiful three-bladed spinner bait. I called him back and asked him how he had missed it. Jan explained that he hadn't. "The barb is rusted off." I looked at the spinner bait and hung it back up in the tree to rust away. The hook on a spinner bait is molded to the lure, so there was no way to fix it.

Plastic lures often have a very durable finish, so I never found myself doing much more than re-hooking and cleaning them if my lazy nature induced me to do anything to them at all. For really beat-up lures, however, I invented a special restoration process. About 15 years ago, I took up and almost immediately gave up the hobby of embedding objects in clear plastic. (You've probably seen the key chains and paperweights with embedded scorpions and whatnot.) The stuff is called "casting resin" and is mixed with a drop or two of hardener before it is poured into a mold. I would give a lure a single coat of enamel paint, let it dry, and then mix up a small batch of casting resin and its hardener. I would brush the resin right over the dry enamel and let it cure overnight. The next day, the plug would have the glassy, hard finish of a professionally-manufactured one —with a lot of unprofessional brush marks. I only did this a couple of times because I am not a very good or meticulous craftsman, but others might be interested in trying it.

***

Well, that's hardly a touch of what I wanted to say about fishing lures. I wish I had time to tell all about them and the millions of memories they evoke. I never told about the amazing Ford Fender trolling rig, or the Castmaster spoon or the Spinrite spinner or how I found the perfect pool for fishing in Minnesota near the Mississippi River headwaters and how the entire Mississippi River used to go through a pipe and how I used to take a canoe through that pipe and come bursting out onto the pool and how the deer flies could run you right out of there. I never got the chance to tell how the water of the pristine Lake Itasca glowed blue but that the blue was only in your mind and all the photos you took came out gray. Oh, there's a lot left to say about fishing lures all right.

I don't fish as much as I used to. I'm just too busy and I also have begun to feel sorry for the fish. The more I look at the critters we share the world with, the more convinced I am that there is next to nothing between us and them except for maybe algebra or western swing guitar or something. But I still have the lures and the memories and my only problem is trying to get them all down on paper.

BIRD WATCHING IN PATAGONIA, ARIZONA

THE WEB—MY TRUCK—THE TUNA, FRUIT, AND BEER
DIET—THE HIGHWAY TO TUCSON—THE SONORAN
DESERT ENDS—SALOONS, KARAOKE, AND LOCAL
YOKELS—THE PRESERVE—PHAINOPEPLAS AND
MISTLETOE—RAP ON BINOCULARS—THE
HUMMINGBIRD FEEDERS—WRONG WAY TOM

I was on the web looking at the Maricopa Audubon Society's page when I saw that on July 29, 2000 there would be a trip to the southern Arizona town of Patagonia, population 200. I knew the place was renowned for its varied bird species and my friends Greg and Dana had been there a million times. I figured it was time I made plans to go down myself to knock off a few life listers.

I told Greg and Dana and they wanted to go but couldn't, so I phoned the trip leader and got on the list of participants alone. This meant that I had agreed to meet the people at the Nature Conservancy's preserve in Patagonia at 7:00 AM on a Sunday morning.

Patagonia is three hours from my home in Chandler and since I am incapable of getting up at 4:00 in the morning for a drive that far, I knew I would have to go down the day before and spend the night. I used the web again, found the only hotel in town, the Stage Stop Inn, and made a 55-dollar reservation. Greg and Dana told me the place had a lounge and there were a couple of saloons down the street. Greg always likes to crack a beer to toast the conclusion of any day's bird watching, and I am always happy to join him.

I made arrangements for my dog Noodles to be cared for and headed down towards Tucson on Interstate 10 at two in the afternoon. It just so happened that I was especially equipped for such a trip as I had very recently purchased a year 2000 Nissan Frontier pick-up with six cylinders, five gears, and four full-sized doors. It was very SUV-like and I felt fairly safe in the thing until I learned that these high-off-the-ground machines roll too easily. One bump from some careless bum on the road and my truck could turn over on the highway. I got the safety stats on my truck and was not happy with what I read. My brand new cruiser was a bowling ball.

I put a cooler on the back seat. It was loaded with pop and beer and some apples and pears. The apples and pears were to help me lose weight. An ectomorph and barely five feet eight inches tall, I knew it was time to do something when I began to push 200 pounds and so I had recently gone on a tuna, fruit, and beer diet and the trip was no occasion to go off of it. The diet, which I invented myself, is simple and effective: you can drink all of the beer you want and eat all of the tuna and fruit you want. That's it. Now, the tuna has to be packed in water instead of oil and technically the beer should be light beer.

The beauty of the diet is that you give up so little for it and it contains absolutely no fat. You can also more easily add exercise to it than with normal diets. This is because you can exercise and have a beer at the same time. It's a wonderful incentive. I go out to my patio and get on the running machine. It's as hot as hell out there, but I have a big fan hooked up that blows air on me. I also have a beer to cool me off and to give me the inclination to go out there and run. It's like my friend Jan's entrepreneurial dream: he wants to have his own bar and grill—only he'll have washing machines and dryers in it so everyone can have a beer while they do their laundry. The principle is essentially the same.

I don't like the drive to Tucson. Interstate 10 is way too narrow and there is a steady barrage of huge trucks barreling back and forth between Phoenix and Tucson. In addition, the scenery is unremarkable, if not unattractive. For a better view you can take 89 south, the Tom Mix Highway. There's a lot of chain fruit cholla along it and it's quite scenic. On the side of the road is a memorial to Tom Mix because he got killed there speeding like a fool in a convertible and crashing into an arroyo. A heavy suitcase in the car came loose in the crash and bashed his brains in. The suitcase is on display in the Tom Mix Museum in Dewey, Oklahoma.

As I drove I tried to pay attention and not let my usual spatial confusion set in. I stayed on I-10 and didn't foolishly get off it for some reason. The fact is, I have no sense of direction and can get lost anywhere at any time. I am simply brain dead with regard to my bearings. I admit it. I almost always make a wrong turn and wind up having to turn around and drive clean back to wherever I goofed up. Because of this, my own nickname for myself is Wrong Way Tom. This disorientation was a particularly dangerous problem for me many years ago when I became a pilot. In fact, when I went up for my test flight with the FAA guy, he told me to fly to a power tower on the map, but I couldn't find it and got lost. Finally he said, "All right, enough! Turn to three six zero degrees. You've been flying around in circles for twenty-five minutes!"

Highway 83 had rolling hills covered with green ocotillos. This, I realized, was no longer my familiar Sonoran Desert. Southeastern Arizona looks like no Arizona you ever saw. It's a mix between Nebraskan-like rolling hills and low chaparral and a touch of scraggly jungle. I hadn't seen any birds along the drive save one turkey vulture, but now I saw feathery movement on the roadside and birds that headed for the bushes and looked like towhees. There wasn't time to get a good enough look to identify them. A big bushy-tailed rock ground squirrel darted in front of my truck and I ran clean over him; I didn't dare swerve enough to avoid him. I looked in my rear view mirror and he was gone. Evidently the tires had missed him and he got nothing worse than the fright of his life.

From Sonoita, Arizona I got on 82 south to Patagonia and arrived in town a short time later. I was surprised at how easy the trip had been. Wrong Way Tom had made it without a hitch. A sign directed me to the Stage Stop Inn and I parked out front and went inside where I had to ding the bell to rouse the clerk. She was Hispanic and young and told me that the restaurant closed at nine and opened at seven. Shoot, I thought. No coffee for breakfast; I had to be down the road at the preserve at seven sharp. I should have brought my own coffee-making gear.

Outside the hotel, barn swallows were everywhere. I looked at them through my binoculars and then went back to the room. It was after five and instead of walking around and doing any bird watching I decided to check out the Lounge. I figured there would be bird watching galore tomorrow. Besides, it was Miller time.

The bartender told me that there were some one-thousand people in the surrounding area and that they didn't often show up at the Stage Stop Lounge. The lounge, he says, was for the convenience of the hotel patrons, but a lot of them were bird watchers and they didn't drink much. "Just a few GT's occasionally." I asked him what a GT was and learned that it was a gin and tonic.

"You sell much of that Bacardi 151, here?" I asked him.

"I won't mix drinks with it," he replied. "It's too dangerous. I just use it for flaming drinks."

I downed the rest of my beer.

"Hey," he said. "Let me make you a flaming Dr. Pepper."

He got a short, none-too-clean glass—like a cafeteria milk glass—and pumped it full of low grade beer from the tap. Then he filled a shot glass with root beer schnapps and set the two in front of me. From the bottle of Bacardi 151 he poured the tiniest bit of high test rum on top of the schnapps and set it on fire. The flame burned weakly. "Drop the shot-glass in the beer!" he ordered.

I picked up the shot glass of flaming schnapps and dropped it in. There was a ploop! and beer cascaded over the rim of the glass; I knew it would. The beer glass was too full.

"It's supposed to spill," he told me, though he didn't offer any good reason why. Properly mixed and scorched, this drink was supposed to taste like Dr. Pepper.

I drank what was left in the glass. The beer was warm and flat and the rum had spilled out and I realized that root beer schnapps didn't go with beer on the best day it ever had. Not only was it the dumbest drink I ever had, but it tasted awful as well.

"Yummy," I said.

I chatted with the bartender a bit longer. He made references to people with grudges against each other around these parts. He also said he knew how to bring business to this lounge but implied that there were forces at work against him. Patagonia: scenic, peaceful, quiet ...but with a terrible secret. I thought.

I turned to the bar TV and saw a show with a DJ playing recorded music for a bunch of dancing teens. I remarked that it was a shame that high school kids didn't have live bands at their dances. I said that in the 1960s we used to always have local bands from the various high schools who would audition to play at each dance and that we would have laughed ourselves sick at the thought of some DJ up there flipping records for us.

The bartender (so *contraire!*) explained that it was easy to become a second-rate DJ, but to be a good one took a lot of experience. I concurred and lamented that the same was true of professional wrestlers, psychics, and chiropractors, but then it was time to go. The bartender said that the Wagon Wheel was the place to be tonight and that it was just down the road, so off I went.

Outside, a big cool breeze was blowing. The weather was quite a bit nicer here than in Chandler. There was a grass-bordered sidewalk through a kind of park and to the left an establishment called "The Big Steer Bar." I walked over and looked in. It was kind of a rough joint, but I pushed open the door and stepped inside anyway and took a seat at the bar.

There was an older Hispanic guy in there with a cowboy hat and a bunch of guys with tape measures on their belts. A Springer spaniel lay on the floor. He looked up and checked me out, staring at me for five or six seconds before lying back down to sleep. The barmaid, in her forties, was wearing a long skirt, a tie-dyed shirt, and a concho belt. I ordered a *Pacífico* and she brought it to me with two dried-up wedges of lime. I guess tradition in Patagonia called for lime with each *Pacífico*, the way it used to always be with *Tecate* in Mexico.

There was an Anglo couple in the bar in their forties and they announced that they had been in love for nineteen years and were finally getting hitched. The Hispanic guy came over and embraced them both.

The TV above the bar blared with a show about some black city kids raising domestic pigeons called flights. They were waging "pigeon wars," a sport where you send your flock of pigeons out to lure the other guy's birds back to your coop. When you've got his birds in your coop, you hold them for ransom. I watched for a while until the beer was gone and then I left for the Wagon Wheel.

The bartender at the Stage Stop Lounge was right; the Wagon Wheel was the place to be. It was full of people but I managed to get a good place at the bar. A girl was setting up a karaoke machine and I quickly went over and signed my name with the number of the tune I wanted to sing: "Mack the Knife." A few people got ahead of me.

Back at the bar I sipped a beer and looked the joint over. The bar itself was made entirely of varnished pine. The walls and ceiling of the room were covered with harnesses and saddles and old rifles and flintlocks and stuffed animals. There was a Red-Tailed Hawk posed as if attacking its prey, a few hapless deer staring from the wall, a gigantic elk's head, a pheasant, a ram, a ferret—I counted ten animals in all.

The crowd was a mix of Hispanic, Native American, and Anglo and they were aged 21 to 81 I guessed. The couple next to me were getting on in years. They both sat drinking beer and chain-smoking. The man had a mottled, almost piebald complexion and thick head of gray hair with that yellow tinge some older guys get. The woman, his wife I presumed,—to whom he rarely spoke—was wrinkled and bony with age.

To my right were two younger guys. One had a good-natured smile and wore one of those cowboy hats that seems kind of broken in the middle so that rain would pour off of it front and back without even getting the guy's shirt wet. The other guy was odd-looking and short. He didn't look too swift to state it bluntly. He too wore a cowboy hat, and it had little guitar pins on it—you know, those tiny pewter replicas of guitars. On his

107

belt he wore a pretty wicked-looking knife. "I love Tucson," I heard him tell his friend. "But I can't afford to live there."

In all, the people reminded me of the clientele in the Vine at Rural and Apache in Tempe. Slightly weird-looking. But why not? This whole place was a little weird; full of stuffed critters and cowboy tack. There was a frog in the urinal too—a plastic one, of course. I supposed it was there to keep things fun and interesting and make sure everyone was on the mark so to speak. The guys at the bar laughed about the frog. "Well," one of them said as he slid off of the bar stool. "I guess I'll go visit Mr. Frog."

"Give him my warmest regards," I said.

The karaoke started and several people did their songs before it was my turn. Normally shy, I had no fear of singing in front of this drunken crowd. My only worry was that they didn't have the original Bobby Darin version of "Mack the Knife" on the machine. There was another version floating around karaoke circles and it didn't sound even half as good. Luckily, this time they had the good one.

The song changes key at least three times but it is just a great number to choose for karaoke. You can even sing it like Satchmo if you like and aside from the key changes and the four-measure note you have to hold at the end, it is very forgiving. I did a real good job and got a fine applause. In fact, a couple of people came out of their seats to shake my hand and punch me in the arm. It was Darin's arrangement actually; I'm not that hot a singer.

The guy in the cowboy hat next to me actually had a good voice, but he picked some countrified thing to sing. I complimented him on the job he did. The karaoke was all so jolly and everyone joined in; even the old guy next to me went up and sang.

Soon enough, however, I was ready to leave. I don't like staying up late. I had had my beer and sung my song, and now I was hungry, sick of tuna, and ready to cheat on the diet, but I realized it was 8:50 and the clerk at the hotel said the restaurant closed at nine. I'd never make it. I decided to have something to eat at the bar.

I ordered a Philly Cheese Steak Sandwich and fries, and oh, what a mountain of fries it was! Calorie city. I ate it all and didn't feel guilty because I hadn't had a real meal in more than a week so it was time. Let me say this: I love American food. The bars, pubs, cafes, and restaurants of America have it down to a science. The lowliest dive can provide a good tasty feed anywhere in this country. Try ordering something to eat in a similar cantina in Mexico. Barf!

It took me a while still to get out of the joint. There was but one barmaid for this whole mob and she had my credit card and it took her forever to get back to me so I could cash out. I finally paid up and split.

On the way back I passed the Big Steer Bar and noticed a fresco on the outside wall—a painting of some floozy, drink in hand. Standing next to it was another floozy—a real one—a young thing all painted up and dressed in floozy clothes. She was with a normal-looking person, so perhaps she was in a play or advertising or something. I didn't ask. I got back to my room, did 30 sit-ups, and went to bed.

The phone rang at six o'clock. It was the wake-up call I had requested. I went over to the preserve, which was only a five-minute drive and saw a bunch of cars and ten or twelve people hanging around. We made some quick introductions and then the Nature Conservancy guy came over and gave us a little talk. Mostly he just told us about the relationship of the Conservancy with the townies and things like that. He also warned us of chiggers and to stay out of the tall grass.

We stood at the edge of a wide meadow just beyond which was a huge meandering stand of giant cottonwoods. Some of these trees were over 100 feet tall and very old.

A lark sparrow jumped into a scraggly bush a few feet in front of us, and beyond—in the meadow— Cassin's kingbirds flew back and forth between bushes and scags. We all looked at them hard, hoping there might be a rare thick-billed kingbird among them. A pair of hooded orioles scared the lark sparrow out of the bush and everyone's binoculars focused in on the brightly colored male.

Far across the field—at the border of the woods—a yellow-billed cuckoo sailed along and alighted in a tree. That bird was a new one for me, and I added its name to the list in my notebook just under the hooded oriole. Then I drew a five-pointed star next to it to show that it was a life lister.

There was a trail through the meadow leading into the cottonwoods, and our group slowly moved down it. Phainopeplas were everywhere and we talked about how even the most spectacular of birds becomes a "trash bird" if there are too many of them around. Such was the case with phainopeplas on this trip. You'd see movement in the trees and raise your binoculars to your eyes only to lower them with a disappointed frown and say, "Just a phainopepla." But the phainopepla is one of the most beautiful birds of all. For those who may be unfamiliar with them, imagine a lean cardinal dipped in the blackest of paint from crest to tail. Give him a narrow bill and two blood-red rubies for eyes. Then add a startling patch of white on each wing that appears only in flight, and you'll have an idea of what the bird looks like. More than once a person has seen my binoculars and come up excitedly to say, "We just saw this bird that looked like a black cardinal!"

"Phainopepla," I answer immediately.

Phainopeplas are silky flycatchers of the arid Southwest. At certain times of year they feed upon poisonous mistletoe berries. During these times, their stomachs shrink to the size of the berries and they process them one after another by swallowing them and squeezing the pulp and seeds out of their bellies and into the intestines and, rather quickly then, into the outside world again. Mistletoe berries don't have much nutritional value, so the birds have to eat an awful lot of them.

A curious drama plays out when the remains of the berries pass through the bird. Mistletoe berries are very sticky. (In fact, people used to use them to make birdlime.) When the sticky seeds that fall from the phainopepla adhere to the limbs of a mesquite tree, the tree knows it and starts a process of self defense by excreting a kind of sap under the seed that raises it above the bark. At the same time, the seed begins its attack by sending out a root-like shoot downward toward the surface of the limb. The tree raises the seed and the seed counterattacks by lengthening the shoot and the race is on. If it rains before the shoot reaches the bark, the seed is washed away and the tree wins the race. If not, the seed will root itself there and a parasitic clump of mistletoe will grow on the limb of the mesquite tree.

We saw yellow-breasted chats when we got into the woods and the occasional white-breasted nuthatch crawling upside down over and under the limbs high in the cottonwood trees. I was a little surprised to see the nuthatches there. I always felt that they were high-altitude birds.

In a clearing overlooking the stream, I spotted a lazuli bunting and everyone rushed over to look. The lazuli bunting is always a welcome sight—or at least the turquoise male is; the drab female is likely to go unnoticed. There were acorn woodpeckers and Gila woodpeckers, red-shafted flickers and summer tanagers in the woods. Hopping on the ground was a small bird with a dark spot on its breast. "Song sparrow," I announced.

"It's a Bewick's wren" someone said.

"But it has a spot on its breast," I protested.

"Well, then it's a Bewick's wren with a spot on its breast."

I looked again and had to admit it looked an awful lot like a Bewick's wren. But what was with the spot?

That wasn't the last misidentification I would make that day. A while later, we were at the edge of a clearing and someone shouted, "Gray Hawk!" I looked through my binocs and caught a gray bird in the field of view. "I've got him," I said as I watched the bird whirl in the intense, magnified blue of the clear sky.

"He's gone," I heard someone say.

"I've still got him!" I replied excitedly. A gray hawk was a rare bird after all.

"No you haven't."

I lowered my binoculars and saw that I had been looking at a big, bull goose Cassin's kingbird fluttering up there.

"Oops," I said.

The trail ended at another stream overlook. There we spotted a blue grosbeak and another male lazuli bunting. We got a warbling vireo there too, although I felt it looked a little chubby for one and I never saw the characteristic white eye line. I wrote him down on my list anyway.

We all sat on some logs and loafed a bit. One of the guys was an former US Air Force F-15 pilot and he and another guy talked about birds and planes. The girl in front of me had a pair of Swarovski 10 X 42 roof prisms and she let me try them out. I focused on a tree that had fallen across the stream. Through the binoculars, the tree looked huge and the view was brighter than that of my Swift Audubon 8.5 X 44 porros. These binocs had some fine optics. Just the same, the image shook quite a lot and the field of view was only 350 feet or something—too narrow for my taste.

Let me clarify the above with some pertinent facts about binoculars. The "10" in "10 X 42" is the power of the binoculars. Simply stated, a pair of ten-power binoculars make a bird look ten times as big as he is. The "42" is simply the diameter in millimeters of the objective lenses—you know, the big end of the binoculars. The bigger this number, the larger the lenses and the more light collected. The term "roof prism" refers to how the light is sent through the binoculars. I have no idea what goes on inside, but there are basically two types of binocs: roof prisms and porros. The position of the prisms in porros imposes the standard binocular shape we are all so accustomed to seeing. The placement of the prisms in roof prism binocs, however, results in quite a different shape, and it allows the user to look straight through the binoculars without the offset eyepieces of the familiar-looking porro glasses. Imagine taping two toilet paper tubes together and looking through them and you'll get the idea of how roof prism binoculars are shaped.

A lot of people think that the higher the power, the better the binoculars. This is simply untrue. Bird watchers are the best experts in binoculars and they almost always use from seven to ten power—rarely lower and almost never higher. Eight power is ideal in my opinion. If you get beyond ten, you'll begin to need a tripod to steady the image. The birds will seem to jump around so much through those glasses that you'll have real trouble identifying them. Look at it this way:

Imagine you've got a 40-power telescope on a tripod precariously focused on a distant star and a pair of hand-held seven-power binoculars. Look at the star with the binoculars for a while and then take the telescope off of the tripod, hold it in your hands, and try to do the same. Which device do you think will give you a quicker, clearer, easier look at the star? You guessed it. Bigger ain't better.

The difference between ten-power and eight-power, while quite noticeable, will probably never make the difference in whether or not you can identify a bird. Lots of people love ten power, however, because of the satisfying, almost addictive size of the image. But they pay a price for that—and not just in a more wobbly, jumpier image; they sacrifice field of view.

My swift Audubon 8.5 X 44s have a whopping 430-foot field of view. This means that at 1000 yards, I can see 430 feet left and right—as well as up and down. It also means that I have an easier view; it's easy to get a bird in my sights with 430 feet to work with. Locating birds with a narrower field of view takes more effort and your eye and mind get tired faster trying to do so.

If you plan to buy binoculars, there's another thing to be aware of. After about 250 dollars you are not necessarily getting better optics; the difference between my 300-dollar glasses and a pair of 800-dollar nitrogen-purged roof prisms is almost all in weather proofing and shock resistance. The actual optics in my binoculars are virtually unmatched at any price.

Of course, there are other features that might be included in the 800-dollar package—like close focus. I can only focus if something is at least 13 feet away, but my friend Dana has expensive roof prisms and they allow her a close focus of just six feet. This is great if you're a butterfly watcher, or if you're very tall and a bird lands on your shoe, or if there are towhees hopping around under the bushes a few feet away. A close view can be spectacular, but there's got to be a price for it; you'll sacrifice something—field of view—whatever. There's always a trade-off with any special binocular feature.

Most people don't realize what a tremendous difference good binoculars make. I didn't know that myself until I upgraded to my Swift Audubons. I can't even see through my old binoculars now. How I ever used them I'll never know. So, if you want to take up bird watching, get some good birding binocs—and don't ask some hunter in the sporting goods section of Walmart or Popular Surplus for advice. They don't know diddle about binoculars. Ask some bird watchers. Over the past sixty years they have put more demands on optics than anyone else on earth and are the real reason that binoculars have evolved into the quality instruments that they have.

Three final suggestions: 1.) Don't buy any binoculars with the little rocker arms that you focus with. If they were a good idea, you'd see them on the 1500-dollar models, but you don't. 2.) Don't buy any instant focus binoculars unless you are so gullible that you believe in magic wands and fairy godmothers. 3.) Don't buy any binoculars with a zoom. You're not going to make a movie; you're going to go bird watching for Christ's sake, so pick a power from seven to ten like I told you and forget about a zoom.

There were a few things that were unsatisfactory about this bird walk. One was that it took us a solid three hours to hike a quarter of a mile into the woods. We spent five hours in essentially the same place and I had no idea that we would do that or else I would have brought some water with me. I had anticipated marching into the riparian area, knocking off some birds and then marching out in a half hour or so to caravan in our cars to the next birding area. That didn't happen. Instead we lounged around for five long hours and only then went somewhere else—to the humming bird feeders in a private residence a minute or two drive from the preserve.

The people who owned the house charged nothing for the privilege of sitting in their yard. All they asked for was some "sugar money" donations so they could fill the feeders. I left them five bucks in the coffee can they had nailed to the fence.

It was all a nice set-up. There were ten big feeders with numbers on each so you could yell, "Violet-crowned on feeder four!" (Instead of "There's a violet-crowned on that half empty feeder sort of second from the end—no... no—the left end!" or something like that.) Hummingbirds swarmed around the feeders like bees.

We saw five species of hummers and I was happy to be reaquainted with the rufous hummingbird again. It was an old friend from my youth when I rouged cotton in the fields from Wickenburg to Safford. I have dates for him as far back as August of 1971. I didn't get to see the blue-throated hummingbird, however, which my computer tells me I had seen once on May 27, 1973, but I didn't mind; I had had enough bird watching for the day.

Despite the long trip, the bird list was pretty unimpressive and quite a bit disappointing. I had only a couple of life listers (indicated below by an asterisk), and the count for the day was a measly 39 listed here in taxonomic order:

1. Turkey Vulture
2. White-winged Dove
3. Mourning Dove
4. Yellow-billed Cuckoo*
5. Broad-billed Hummingbird
6. Violet-crowned Hummingbird*
7. Black-chinned Hummingbird
8. Anna's Hummingbird
9. Rufous Hummingbird
10. Acorn Woodpecker
11. Gila Woodpecker
12. Northern Flicker
13. Western Wood-Pewee
14. Black Phoebe
15. Vermilion Flycatcher
16. Ash-throated Flycatcher
17. Brown-crested Flycatcher
18. Cassin's Kingbird
19. Warbling Vireo
20. Barn Swallow
21. White-breasted Nuthatch
22. Bewick's Wren
23. Curve-billed Thrasher
24. Phainopepla
25. Yellow Warbler
26. Common Yellowthroat
27. Yellow-breasted Chat
28. Summer Tanager
29. Western Tanager
30. Lark Sparrow
31. Song Sparrow
32. Black-headed Grosbeak
33. Blue Grosbeak
34. Lazuli Bunting
35. Brown-headed Cowbird
36. Hooded Oriole
37. House Finch
38. Lesser Goldfinch
39. House Sparrow

We had planned to go to a roadside rest area where people had seen the rose-throated becard, but I didn't bother. I knew the bird had not been seen this season and it was a waste of time. I bid everyone *adiós* and got in my truck and headed back to Chandler.

I passed Karchner Caverns State Park on the way, and I pulled in to take a look. All the tours were booked for the day, but I got a brochure and left. Then, a fear struck me and I turned back to the State Park and asked the ranger where I was.

"You've got a good hour back to Tucson," she said —but I already knew what had happened. The State Park was right next to Benson and that meant I was thirty miles east of where I was supposed to be, a fact that translated as sixty miles of unnecessary driving. Dang!

Wrong Way Tom had done it again.

FIRST AND SECOND RETURNS TO ITASCA

GRANDFATHERED IN—MY DAD THE BIOLOGIST—
CISCOS, STICKLEBACKS, AND NORTHERNS—LIGHTING
STROBE—WIND

Thomas Wolfe said you can't go back, but he was wrong. I know that he was wrong because I myself have gone back to Lake Itasca in Minnesota twice and it worked out just fine.

I found that nothing had changed when I returned. Everything was exactly as I remembered it and exactly as I left it with each stone on the shore and each trail in the woods and each turn in the stream perfectly in place just as it was 20 years and even 35 years before. And what's more, I was grandfathered in—I still owned the place and no one stepped up to dispute the claim. No one wanted to, and quite possibly no one dared.

My father was a limnologist—an aquatic biologist —who was hired every year to teach at the University of Minnesota's biological station in Itasca State Park. Because of this, I spent my summers on Lake Itasca, a big, pristine tree-lined water world of bass and walleyes, where the days were long and lazy and the living was just plain fat.

Itasca is no phony lake with its population of bass and bream carefully managed like the carp and catfish in a Texas stock tank. No, Itasca is a real lake with its own breeding schools of everything from ciscos to sticklebacks to northern pike as long as your leg—heck, as long as both of your legs.

Itasca is mostly a sun-drenched pool of azure, but it can also be a windy expanse of gray waves leaping high and frothing white. And when a thunderstorm rolls over the lake, the lightning creates a constant, even strobe that makes people walking around look as though they were at a 1960s acid rock concert. If the wind really kicks up, trees as big as California's giant sequoia, "the General Sherman" topple around the lake and across the single park road. In the morning, I have seen the rangers with big power saws cutting up the trees so that cars can get through. But as I said, Itasca is mostly a sunny, mild place perfect for anybody's summer.

FIRST RETURN 1987

A New Green Van—Eagles Nest—Cheyenne, Lusk, Branches—The Lonely Plains, Clementine —The Center of the Continent

In the summer of 1987 it occurred to me that I had not been back to Itasca in better than twenty years. I pitched in with my brother Steve and bought a gigantic ice cream green Ford Van and set out one day to retrace the old trips north, relive a little of the past, and do some fishing.

We recorded everything on the trip. The van got 16.3 miles per gallon. (God, it was a beautiful machine.) Our total mileage was 4,305 miles, the KOA in Nebraska cost eleven dollars, I read *Space Prison* by Tom Godwin, we crossed the meandering Platte River four times while driving in the same direction.

We stayed off the interstate for much of the trip and were able to see real places with real personalities instead of the freeway fringe of tract housing and the like. The small towns on the road to Itasca interested me. I'd try to imagine living in such places and I'd wonder what it would be like to have my horizons dragged in so much closer by living in, say, Eagles Nest, a tiny town on a big lake between Taos and Raton.

The trip to Itasca is full of the images of the towns along the way. Cheyenne must be the smallest capital of any state. It sure looked small to me anyway. It rests on the dreary, rather shaggy western plains—what is left of the great prairie frontier. We drove from there on to Chugwater, Shawnee, Lost Springs, Keeline, and Lusk. I was especially taken by Lusk because it was so clean and neat, and small though it was, it had its own historical museum. What's more, just outside of town, it had branches—those yard-wide streams, three feet deep that wander through boggy meadows. I always used to think of Vermont when I thought of branches because my mom used to fish in them there. I had also once heard of a folk recipe for a mixed drink of some kind that called specifically for branch water. No other type of water would do.

As you drive deeper and deeper into the center of the continent, a loneliness creeps up on you. I attribute much of the feeling to the openness of the plains, the emptiness. As a very young child I remember looking out the windows of the family station wagon to see a few old abandoned houses standing out on the plains a hundred, two hundred miles from anywhere and feeling a overwhelming sense of sadness and despair. Who could have lived in such places and how could they have stood it? For some reason, a line from the song "Clementine" would always come to me at such sights. When I was a child, they were the saddest words I knew: "You are lost and gone forever. Dreadful sorry..."

In 1987 I felt the weight of the continent heavy upon me as we drove further toward its center. But it didn't depress me in the slightest. This time it was just one more interesting aspect of traveling north—back to Itasca.

SECOND RETURN 2000

The Perfect Vacation—Sonny—Night Driving, Bastards with Bright Lights—Monster Music

I've got a new system for a trim but perfect vacation. Plan it for five days. That's the secret. Look, you've got a day of traveling there and one back and then three solid days and four solid nights to do what you set out to do. It's perfect. It's what my brother and I did on our second return to Itasca in the summer of the year 2000. And this time we brought Sonny, Steve's 9-year-old son, a precocious, rambunctious towhead.

Naturally we didn't drive; Minnesota would be too far away to fit the five-day schedule. We flew to Minneapolis on an Air Bus, a European 737 knock-off that rattled and groaned the whole way and yawed quite frighteningly on take-off and landing. My brother kept yelling, "Top rudder! Put some top rudder on it!"

When we got to Minneapolis, we rented a car. In front of us we had a road trip of better than 250 miles to get to Itasca. Since the plane landed in the late afternoon, that meant night driving, which I hate.

Two-lane night driving sometimes seems to me like something out of the past. It's a forties or fifties-ish kind of endeavor when everyone used to risk their necks more than they do today on crummy two-lane roads and no one thought twice about having no seat belt or driving at night in the rain. I'd forgotten what it was like. Here's exactly what happens:

I

"Oh, that bastard! That bastard won't dim his lights. Well, I'll flash my brights to let him know. Ah, he dimmed them. Thank you—jerk. I'm half blinded, you dumb bastard...

II

"Oh, another bastard! Another bastard who won't dim his lights. I'll flash my brights. Oh, he flashed his brights back at me—aagg! My eyes! His headlights were ALREADY dimmed! Well your dims are too damned bright, you dumb bastard. Get 'em fixed...

III

"Hey, who's this bastard? He's flashing his brights at ME! My brights aren't on, you dumb bastard. You want to see brights? Well, here they are! Hey, they dimmed! My brights *were* on! SORRY! SORRY!"

Sonny sat in the back seat and it was my job to play the blaring tapes he wanted to hear on the cassette machine on the dash. The tapes were out-of-season Halloween monster tunes with Elvira and other grade B performers singing. They posed a safety hazard, as they were driving me crazy. I seemed immersed in a world of roaring darkness punctuated by the occasional blinding flashes from the headlights of oncoming cars, but Steve talked me into letting Sonny play his tapes anyway.

I drove clean to Bemidji passing through a thousand small towns on the way and seeing little more of them than what the headlights revealed at the side of the road.

FIRST RETURN 1987

GERMAN BROWNS AND PARK BENCHES—ROOSTER TAILS DRAGGED WITH THE CURRENT—POLISHED WRITING—FREE CAMPING—MID CONTINENTAL SUNSET—FISHING AT OAHE DAM—MOONEYES AND WALLEYES—WE GET SKUNKED!

Steve and I pulled our new van into Spearfish, South Dakota on June 9, 1987. Spearfish is a nice university town with a trout stream that runs around and through it. You can fish for German browns from half of the city park benches in Spearfish . We caught a few good ones by casting Rooster Tail brand spinners upstream and reeling them back. (If you know anything, you don't cast downstream when you're fishing in a fast-moving brook. The rushing water will make your spinner spin like crazy as you reel it in, but no self respecting trout will believe anything natural is moving against the current that way. And he would have to beat the current himself to go after it.)

As I mentioned, we kept copious notes in a journal during the trip and some of the entries suggest that we had plenty of leisure time to polish the writing. For example, on June 9, 1987 I wrote:

After looking over the town of Belle Fourche and its big, icky fishless reservoir, my associate Stephen and I decided to revisit Spearfish, South Dakota and perhaps inquire of the local residents what lodgings could be procured. Being possessed of shy demeanor and seeing as we did that such questioning might be a bit intrusive and of an unseemly character and, indeed, of questionable intent, Stephen and I deigned to spare our northern countrymen the vexation planned earlier and instead consulted—both of us—with considerable concerned interest the literature supplied us by the tourism department in hopes that we might independently acquire the needed information that would enable us—if only briefly—to enjoy the campground facilities available locally. We were even willing to pay.

In one of our pamphlets was mentioned a campground facility near the fishing stream in town, and Stephen, having read and relayed this information to me, was very keen on going there at once while at the same time seeming most mightily interested in our arriving there without delay and being, in addition, not a little anxious to be off quickly.

Instead, however, we left Spearfish and spent the night in Pierre, where there was free camping on the Missouri River. (Did I say that Cheyenne was the smallest state capital in the US? Perhaps it is Pierre.) There were black rain clouds in the late afternoon and a big sky filled with pink—almost like an Arizona sunset.

In the morning, we drove the van a couple of miles to Fort Pierre, where we tried to catch some fish in the tailrace waters of Oahe Dam. Many years ago Steve had caught a pair of mooneyes there. Mooneyes are eerie-looking giant minnows with huge yellow, owlish eyes. This was also the same spot where I caught the first fish that I ever caught on a lure. I still have the lure and the fish's jaws. It was a walleyed pike. This time, however, we got skunked, but we didn't mind very much because we had a lot of fun just trying to catch fish and we knew we would do better at Itasca.

SECOND RETURN 2000

SUPER 8—MOTEL 6—BEMIDJI—HOMES ON THE LAKE —"THE WILLOW POPPER"—THE JITTERBUG—SONNY CATCHES A LARGEMOUTH BASS

Bemidji is a half hour north of Itasca and it irked us to have to stay there and commute to the park, but we had little choice; it was the Fourth of July weekend and the Douglas Lodge, a wonderful rustic hotel right on Lake Itasca, was booked solid. For a long time,I had had the dream of staying there. Steve instead had reserved us a room in the Super 8 in Bemidji, but we had a bit of trouble finding it because the bonehead kept

127

calling it a Motel 6 of which there aren't any in Bemidji.

It was late when we arrived there but there were lots of young people walking around town. A loud rock 'n' roll band was playing on the side of the road. Bemidji is a university town on the wild, giant lake of the same name. In the 60s, I remember Lake Bemidji being full of sea planes, but on this trip we saw none.

The next morning, we took a wrong turn on the way out and we had to drive through some neighborhoods. We saw that many people had the shore of Lake Bemidji right in their backyards. In a land of 10,000 lakes this kind of thing is not unusual.

I had made a list of the places I wanted to see again and the things I wanted to do. First of all, I wanted to go down to the dock at the Douglas Lodge. More than 35 years before, I had stood there and watched an obnoxious youth about my age talk about his "Willow Popper."

"Look at that big sunfish," he said. "I'll just put my brand new Willow Popper over near him and he'll see the Willow Popper, and he'll want the Willow Popper, and he'll bite the Willow Popper!"

Willow Popper this, Willow Popper that. I thought the kid must have been brain dead; the Willow Popper was bigger than the stupid fish. Later, I learned that I had misheard; the lure was called a Hula Popper and as I became more experienced with fishing, I grew to like the Hula Popper even less. I had my reasons. However, the same company also manufactured the Jitterbug, which I believe is the finest topwater lure ever made. Before the trip I bought a brand new one and now in the

128

bright sunlight of the year 2000 Sonny came up to me on the dock and said, "Tom, can I borrow your Jitterbug?"

"Sure you can, Sugar Bunny," I replied.

It was public dock with people around and there wasn't much chance of catching anything, but he could give it a try. You never know in Minnesota, and you never know with a Jitterbug.

Steve helped Sonny fasten the lure to the line and gave him instructions. "Just walk it along in front of those lily pads."

A five-pound largemouth bass suddenly appeared from out of the dark watery shadows beneath the Jitterbug, opened its mouth and, inhaled the lure.

The fight was on.

"Don't horse him!" Steve warned. "Whatever you do, don't horse him!"

Sonny horsed the fish up to the dock as Steve threw himself halfway over the boards, grabbed the bass by the lower jaw, and hauled him out of the water. From that moment on, Sonny wore a huge smile that was kept alive by the fact that he continued to out fish both of us consistently throughout the entire trip.

FIRST RETURN 1987

PERCH-COLORED LAZY IKE — THE DEEP DIVIN' JESUS —
A FISHER FOR CHRIST AND A LETTER TO EXACT
VENGEANCE AND REDRESS — BIG NORTHERNS — OLAF'S
— FREE 3.2 BEER — FREE CAMPING — NAGGING
TWELFTH MAGNITUDE HANGOVERS — RACCOONS EAT
OUR PIKE

The van ran like a dream to Fargo/Moorhead and onward to Park Rapids and Itasca. We rented a rowboat when we got there, put Steve's Gamefisher 1.5-horse outboard on it, and started trolling. Steve used a perch-colored Lazy Ike. It was an exact replica of the lure he used as a kid to massacre—I said MASSACRE the walleyes at Itasca. (The original lure is retired and in Steve's archival tackle box at home.)

I used a lure we called the Deep-diving Jesus. We called it that because before the trip Steve bought a fishing lure and when he opened the package there was printed material in there from one Samuel Tyler, Company President urging him to be a "Fisher for Christ." Steve got mad at the proselytizing, which he had every right to do; he'd bought the lure in good faith trusting there would be no strings attached and having been raised, as I was, in a family of pretty devout atheists, he felt the insult perhaps a bit more deeply than others might and believed that redress and restitution were justified and would be exacted at once. He quickly dashed off the following letter:

> Dear Mr. Tyler:
>
> I just bought one of your deep diving plugs. On the very first cast, a fish hit it and broke off the plastic diving lip. This fish was only a small bluegill. As a fellow Christian, how's about a new lure?
>
> Yours in Christ,
>
> Hank Johnson

Steve and I always use the Hank Johnson alias whenever we get up to such shenanigans. Anyway, a few short days later a brand spanking new lure sporting first class postage arrived at Steve's house and we both knew we had a winner—a lure that was surely supercharged with good luck and which we felt blessed to have so fortuitously acquired.

The lure did indeed seem bestowed with grace and good fortune. I hooked a gigantic northern pike on it and added it to the stringer with the fish that Steve had caught on his Lazy Ike. Here's a picture of the fish we caught. That's me holding up the stringer. The big fish in front was caught on the Deep-divin' Jesus.

First Return to Itasca 1987, Hefty Northerns

It was a great day of fishing and afterwards I drove us to Olaf's, the old local bar that all the biologists used to frequent. Now, Steve and I were on the wagon and I had been something of a jogging health nut for some time. The nostalgia, however, was a huge temptation (as most anything is when it is time to fall off the wagon) and so we saddled up to the bar and ordered a couple of frosty 3.2's to toast our success. Yes, this part of Minnesota only served 3.2 beer, but believe me you can get pretty schnockered on it as we were soon to learn.

Olaf had sold the joint a few years earlier and the guy running the bar didn't even want to be there. He himself had sold the place a year ago but part of the contract said he'd have to take it back if the buyer couldn't make a go of it. The buyer flaked out and now the poor guy was back behind the counter with a whimsical expression on his face and a distinct feeling of deja vú as he listened to endless drunks blabbing on and on day in and day out about walleyes and women and trucks. Hey, who says you can't go back?

On this day he decided not even to charge for the beer and so all you had to do was say, "Fill her up!" and he would. To this day I do not understand his action. I do know that everyone drank until last call and no one paid a dime for anything. Nor left a tip neither.

Steve and I pedaled the van back to the campground and as it was late in the evening the station was closed and there was no one to collect our fee. We awoke with nagging twelfth magnitude hangovers and found that the raccoons had raided our cooler and eaten all of the pike. They lay stripped and boned behind the van. I didn't mind, of course. What were we doing carting those pike around anyway?

We packed up and left the campground as early as we could so the ranger wouldn't be there to collect our fee on the way out. This may seem dishonest; it is not. We were grandfathered in—grandfathered, see?—and Steve and I were not about to argue the point with anybody or pay for the privilege of staying in our own place.

SECOND RETURN 2000

PISS POT VISTA—THE CULVERT—SONNY CATCHES CRAPPIES AND A ROCK BASS—THE TEN-FOOT LOG— CIVIL RIGHTS WORKERS

There were other sights on my list that I wanted to see. One was Peace Pipe Vista, a gorgeous overlook of Lake Itasca surrounded by tall white pines. I made the mistake of calling it "Piss Pot Vista," a term that Sonny would repeat every two minutes for the remainder of the trip.

We also had to visit the culvert, a pipe through which the entire Mississippi flowed into a beautiful, fishy pool at the end of which the river continued lazily onward until it turned out of sight to continue through places unknown and mysterious to me.

We went down to the pool and Sonny hooked and landed two black crappies and a strapping red-eyed rock bass. I caught a pike. I always felt that this was the perfect fishing pool as it was possible to catch anything —anything at all—in it.

Upstream are the headwaters of the Mississippi. Before the trip I had come across a picture of my parents newly married I guessed, standing at the headwaters. They lived in Minneapolis at the time and must have driven up.

On this trip, Sonny stood at the same headwaters and cast a little spinner out to catch creek chubs, plumpish sucker-mouthed minnows. At the headwaters is a ten-foot log standing on end. On it is carved the following:

HERE 1475 FT
ABOVE
THE OCEAN
THE MIGHTY
MISSISSIPPI
BEGINS
TO FLOW
ON ITS
WINDING WAY
2552 MILES
TO THE
GULF
OF MEXICO

The log brought back memories because in the 1960s my friends and I committed a small act of vandalism that resulted in a strange twist for me. Late one night, we walked through the woods from the biology station all the way to the headwaters and pushed the log over. The next day we knew the rangers would just set it back up, but I was still a little nervous about the crime when I got up and went to breakfast.

My father sat at the table with me and picked up the morning paper.

"Hmm," he said, looking at the front page. "It looks like there's been some dirty work down in Mississippi."

Holy cow! I thought. It's in the paper? Already? I soon learned, however, that my father was not talking about the Mississippi River. He was reading about the young civil rights workers who were murdered by those redneck cops down in the state of Mississippi.

Although it was the Fourth of July weekend we only had to wait an hour to rent a boat and motor. Minnesota is simply not a very crowded place. We trolled over to the biology station and stopped at the docks. Two professors with Arizona connections were there and both knew my parents. We talked to them and swapped 30-year-old names. They knew most everyone we did. "Oh, Jim Underhill isn't doing too well," one of them said.

We hung around for some time at the docks where I had spent so many happy times fishing. Eastern kingbirds fluttered out across the water catching insects. I'd forgotten all about them. They seemed strangely gaudy with that touch of red and the white fancy, almost lacy border at the end of the tail. One perched on a water craft that we immediately called the Tom Poon II. The original Tom Poon was christened in the 1960s by one of the faculty children who couldn't pronounce "pontoon." The name Tom Poon was not painted on the side as before and it didn't seem to be the same craft, so that's why we called it the Tom Poon II.

I heard a white-throated sparrow in the trees behind the dock and suddenly wanted to do some decent bird watching, but Steve and Sonny were there to fish so we went trolling again instead. We trolled all three days and Sonny caught pike after pike and said, "Eat my dust, you guys!" every time he got one.

We went to the Douglas Lodge to eat and oh what vittles they served! The place smelled somehow like pipe tobacco and cedar. I liked everything about the Douglas Lodge. They even served a nice hoppy Summit Pale Ale. (No 3.2 beer this!) We asked again about rooms and to our surprise learned that there was a vacancy. We immediately drove 30 miles back to Bemidji and checked out of the Super 8. My dream of staying at the Douglas Lodge had come true.

At the Douglas Lodge gift shop we mentioned that we were from Arizona, the woman there said, "Oh, you're the Coles!" She had not seen us in 30 years, but for some reason remembered us. She had lived on the biology station because her father was on the staff and ran the daily operations there. "I never left home, as you can see," she said.

That night, I walked by our part of cabin #1 and saw next to it a room with someone seated in an overstuffed chair reading. I though at first that it was the office, but suddenly I realized that this was an actual reading room. The light shone yellow through the windows and screen door and there was a fireplace and a couch or two inside. This I knew was a low key place torn from the past and I also knew that the perfect book to read there would be one of Edgar Rice Burroughs' or Jack London's adventures—in hardback, of course—one of those old old Grosset and Dunlap books. If you've ever read one, you know that at the end of each is a page that informs you of the following:

"There is a Grosset & Dunlap Book for every mood and for every taste."

FIRST RETURN 1987

THE LUNATIC AT THE PIANO—LEAVING NEBRASKA—A BLOODY WRECK

Steve and I did all we wanted to do in a few days, hopped back in our van and headed home. The trip back had its moments. For instance, in the lobby of a KOA campground in Nebraska was a piano. I sat down and really started banging those horse teeth. I played "Sophisticated Lady" and "The Lullaby of the Leaves" and "Old Man River" and "Willow Weep for Me." Then I played "Danny Boy" and "Martha my Dear" and "Body and Soul." I was having a great time. Soon, however, I noticed that no one in the lobby smiled. No one came over to listen or make a request. In fact, people began to leave the room. Then I noticed a sign— a rather large one, and it was right on the piano music stand directly in front of my nose. It read:

THIS PIANO IS PRIVATE PROPERTY AND NOT FOR PUBLIC USE. THOSE WHO PLAY IT WILL BE ASKED TO LEAVE THE CAMPGROUND.

Then I understood the people's reaction. They saw me as a willful, brass-balled lawbreaker who could give a damn about the sign or anything else. Possibly they

137

reasoned, I was a dangerous lunatic. I, in turn, reasoned that a dangerous lunatic who plays the piano must be even scarier than your regular garden variety dangerous lunatic—kind of the way a sociopath wearing a clown's suit is more frightening by far than a sociopath in a T-shirt, jeans, and sneakers. I decided to stop my performance after that first set and left the lobby humming the Broadway show tunes that I never got the chance to play.

There is little else to note here regarding the trip back in 1987 except to say that I learned that driving out of Nebraska is better than driving into it and that on the way back there was a horrible bloody fatality on a lonely stretch of highway in Northern Arizona, the sight of which haunted me for days and weeks afterward.

SECOND RETURN 2000

MOSQUITOES, DEER FLIES, PRIME RIB, 20 TO 1 RATIO, ANOTHER HEADWATERS, SCHOOLCRAFT ISLAND, SERVICE ROADS

The year 2000 return to Itasca was as perfect a trip as I have ever made. We hardly fought or argued. There were virtually no mosquitoes or deer flies—only wonderfully magical and mysterious fireflies. The weather was sublime. I treated myself to prime rib and endless pale ales and stuffed myself at the lodge with breakfasts of sausage and bacon and ham and eggs over hard and hash browns that contained more butter than potato. We got up early each morning to listen to the loons.

Steve and Sonny agreed to follow my list of places to go and things to do. There were a few lakes on the list and since one in twenty acres of Minnesota is water, there's no great premium on such places and you get the lake to yourself half the time. We went to Squaw Lake, the site of wonderful fishing memories for Steve and me. We went to Elk Lake, whose waters rush into Itasca and so make you suspect that you have found the true headwaters of the Mississippi. (The scientists say no, but still I wonder.) We looked over Lake Mary, too.

As planned on my To Do List, we landed our boat on Itasca's Schoolcraft Island and climbed up its banks through the poison ivy to a forest floor ten or fifteen feet above the level of the lake. There, I was lucky enough to see a red-eyed vireo as we explored the jungly woods on the island. When we got back in the boat, a giant pileated woodpecker flew overhead across the lake and into the trees on the faraway east shore.

We even took the time to walk down the lonely and overgrown service roads in the park as we used to do, and there I saw high in the trees a chestnut-sided warbler.With that, we had exhausted the list and were content to get up early, listen one last time to the loons crying across the lake, and finally drive back to Minneapolis where we hopped on the jet and were home before we knew it.

I know now that I have done away with 20 and 30-year absences from Itasca. The five-day plan makes the trip manageable without eating up the rest of whatever vacation you might have and I have resolved that from now on I will return to Itasca every three years or so.

THIRD RETURN TO ITASCA

WOOD TICKS LEECHES AND DEER FLIES—PARK RAPIDS
—I GET A HAIRCUT—OUR BARTENDERS DRINK ON THE
JOB—THE HEADWATERS BAR—PIZZA AND GIANT
MOSQUITOES—KNIT WITS AT NETTIE'S NET

In July of 2001 my sister Sally and I met in
Minnesota to relive part of our childhood and to get
away from it all. I flew into Minneapolis from Arizona
and she from New Orleans. There we rented a mid-
sized car—an Alero—and headed north to Lake Itasca,
one of the most beautiful places you're likely to see.
What follows is just part of what happened.

I'm not afraid of wood ticks, but I found that Sally
is. I welcome them myself and rather enjoy it on the
rare occasions when they fasten themselves to me and I
have to yank them off. The same goes for leeches,
although they are a lot creepier. I used to fear leeches
until I learned that they never burrow completely into
you and start surfing your bloodstream. Before that,
when I found one on me, I would rip it off and think I
had removed him just before he headed for my liver to
coat himself with human antigens and storm
unchallenged through my system. Sally was afraid of
Lyme disease from the wood ticks. But the ticks we saw
weren't those tiny deer ticks that carry the disease. This
summer the deer flies were the real problem—so much
so that we had to abort one decent walk from the
Douglas Lodge to Mary Lake. They were eating us
alive. And on Squaw Lake (now politically correctly

named Lake Ozawindib), we would try to swim underwater as much as we could because when we surfaced for air, they would be on us in a flash! And they hurt.

It was interesting to see the old sights from the 60s —the Deer Town tourist trap near the town of Park Rapids, Whimpy's hamburger franchises, Fuller's tackle shop, and so on. Minnesota, of course, has a different selection of birds. At the lodge, the hummingbird feeders were alive with ruby-throated hummers, a species not seen in Arizona. The fact is that they are the only eastern species, while Arizona boasts ten or more. Among the many birds we were able to see were the blackburnian warbler, the chestnut-sided warbler, the painted redstart, the purple martin, the chimney swift, the red-eyed vireo, the black duck, and a host of others we don't get to see at home.

I rented a boat with an outboard and Sally and I went trolling. Actually, she went sight-seeing and I trolled for pike. I didn't do very well. I was skunked at the Crappie hole and nothing would strike while I trolled either. Finally, I caught a pike on a jitter bug and Sally netted him—but that was a disappointment too because it was a scrawny pike and I at first thought it was a largemouth bass the way it had smacked that surface plug.

We landed on Schoolcraft Island and I found that Sally liked poison ivy little more than wood ticks. The island was covered with the stuff, and you had to walk through it to get anywhere. Poison ivy doesn't bother me. You can stomp through it and usually nothing happens. The worst I've had was some on the soles of my feet in the sixties—when I didn't wear shoes in the summer. That was actually a good place to have it because you could scratch it with every step you took. I wonder if my old friend Bill Underhill invented his ridiculous "I'm gonna go, go, to the show..." dance from the odd way he walked when he had poison ivy on the bottoms of his feet.

We got rid of the boat and went to the culvert where I just massacred the fish. I would toss in my lure and instantly I would have a pike or a rock bass on the line. The trouble was that the barbs were tearing up the fish. I had to kill one pike with a rock because I simply could not get the lure out of him. It was ghastly. It's really no different from massacring chipmunks—it's just that the chipmunks will SCREAM and fish can't on account of they don't have any lungs. I decided to stop fishing and if I ever did again I would take a pair of pliers and mash the barbs flat. That's what they make you do on the Colorado at Marble Canyon. They don't want you tearing up the trout and if you can't get the hooks out of a fish, you can't "catch and release."

In 1966 Park Rapids was not exactly hip. Back then, I walked down the street and people would spin on their heels to see my hair, which was just a Beatles/surfer cut. I remember kids running up to our car to see where the hell we were from and saying, "Oh, ARIZONA!" If California was a year or two ahead of the times with respect to Arizona, as it always seemed to be, then Arizona was a year or two ahead of Park Rapids.

This trip, however, Sally and I found the new Park Rapids to be a rather hip town and quite a cool place—

rustic and very western in style. Many of the Minnesotan small towns look a lot like Gun Smoke's Dodge City—they seem quite a bit more western—Hollywood style—than most Arizona towns, which are far more Spanish in design. I stopped into a barber shop and got a quick haircut. Sally was patient and I really needed one. More than thirty years ago I was part of a big scene in a barber shop in Park Rapids, and it may well have been this very one. (My father kept telling the barber to cut some more off and the barber would say, "I don't want the boy to be mad at me." Finally he just hacked away and messed up my hairdo. I felt he was just being lazy.) But this time the woman cutting my hair and I had a fine time yacking and yucking. Sally and I then decided to pop in for a beer somewhere.

We found that the Royal Bar was the best place to go; it had a good selection of beer and there was quite a community of Park Rapiders in there—old and young and in the middle of the day. The bartenders in the Royal Bar have a drink every time you order one of your own, a fact that surprised me a great deal. Didn't they have liquor control here? We found that it was standard procedure for the bartenders to drink on the job.

The place was so crowded, however, that we went and hit another joint called Art's Place. Oh, God how low class it looked from the outside—and inside it presented no disappointment. It was a dark, damp joint made for get-down-and-drink drinkin'. Arizonans usually just order beer, but Minnesotans drink a lot of hard liquor in those bars. We had a beer that was absolutely insipid and icky and we left and went back to the Royal, found a place at the bar and had a beer and a nice chat with the drunk bartender. Wood ticks were crawling out of my clothes and Sally wanted to scoot away from me. We didn't stay long. We drove back to Lake Itasca and did an afternoon of sight-seeing .

When we returned to the Douglas Lodge, we were late for dinner. The lodge restaurant had closed and we were not afforded its yummy repast. Now, about a quarter mile from the Lake is the Headwaters Bar where we figured we could get something to eat. They had just had a fire that destroyed most of the kitchen and they had nothing to serve but toaster oven pizza—but it was absolutely excellent! We went in twice for pizza during this third return trip to Itasca. The Headwaters also served good beer—my favorite being the Summit Pale Ale—a hoppy concoction that was close to an India Pale Ale.

In the Headwaters, giant mosquitoes would appear out of nowhere and attack you as you sat at the bar. There was some hole in the wall or something where they were getting in, but no one could find it. It is an exaggeration, but not too great a one, to say that those mosquitoes were as big as mayflies.

The Headwaters used to have a lot more than pizza. A year before, I had ordered prime rib there. A young and reluctant waitress served it to me. I could tell she didn't want to play the role of waitress. It just wasn't in her.

When we asked about other eateries, all the waitresses at the Headwaters said, "Oh ya, ya, the Headwaters is the only place before Park Rapids or Bemidji.." They were wrong. We saw a restaurant/bar on the main highway just three miles from Itasca. It was called Nettie's Net. Late the next afternoon we went over there hoping to have some walleye.

Nettie's Net was owned and operated entirely and exclusively by Knit Wits! They all drank on the job too and they didn't quite look like Minnesotans—don't ask me how, but they were more like New Yorkers and kind of retarded New Yorkers at that. One of them was on our side of the bar and blabbing at the decibel level of a major earthquake. He was in his late forties and perhaps related to all of this clan and he told the filthiest stories. Everybody smiled, young and old, and thought he was charming.

After a long wait, as kind of an afterthought it seemed, the bartender directed his attention to us and we ordered a beer. We didn't want to order food in the place anymore. But we thought we'd make a polite purchase and split. The beers took ages to get to us and the shouting and noise from the patron-owners was deafening.

Nettie was there. I recognized her as the chief cook and bottle washer because she was barking more orders than anybody else. No one paid her the slightest attention. There were at least eight people running the place, and none of them were quite sure if they were working or just partying at the bash they were hosting. You could tell that this was a big night for them by how upbeat and excited they were. They had a live band setting up outside and it was just going to be one big northern Minnesota stomping session.

We went out to see the band. A rough-looking fiftyish man was playing a beat-up Stratocaster through a one-hundred watt Fender amp along with a bass player and a drummer whose drums were miked and ear-splitting. They were banging out some Credence Clearwater Revival standards. The only audience sat fifty feet back in lawn chairs—an older crowd of about six, perhaps relatives of Nettie. The dirt parking lot dance floor in front of the band was empty and I had the feeling not many people were going to show for this gig. Nettie and clan would never know the difference, however; I knew that they would be so hungover the next day they would judge their condition as evidence that the whole project had been a roaring success unmindful of the fact that they had drunk up all of the profits.

I Snore Like a Mother F...—A Drizzly Sky—A Special Smell—Dirt Forest Roads—Giant Cows —Family Homes Built Deep in the Woods— Children's Crayon Drawings—A Note Inside— The Piano in the Stairway—The Loon Song Bed and Breakfast.—A Private Lake

Sally and I had a tiny room in one of the little cabins next to the Douglas Lodge. Sally was concerned that she would get little sleep as she has always said in her irreverent way, "Tom, you snore like a motherfucker!" I don't really know why she describes it in such rough terms because I'm not sure that motherfuckers are especially celebrated for their snoring. I am sure that I snore loudly enough to merit most any such kind of simile. She seemed to be able to sleep well enough on this trip, however.

146

The first day was clear and bright but we awoke on the second to a drizzly sky. I was worried the trip could suffer, but the different weather added some variety to the experience. It doesn't rain much in Arizona and it is interesting to see how the other half lives. There is also a special smell that comes after a rain in a northern forest. It's not the dusty smell of an Arizona shower whose drops make a puff of fine ochre powder rise into the air from the street; Minnesota rain brings on a more peaty fragrance.

The skies had pretty much cleared by the afternoon and we weren't slowed down at all. Our plan for the trip was to hit all of the places that Steve and Sonny and I did the year before and then add some. To this end we decided to go down some dirt forest roads to see what mysteries lay in wait for us.

Thirty-five years before I had gone down such roads with a friend and saw a farm in the distance. My memory has it this way: we stopped the car and looked. There, before our eyes, Giant Cows stood at the end of the road. Giant Cows. They were as tall as houses— taller—their shoulders flush with the roof of the barn— impossibly big. No such cows ever lived. The scene was like something out of a drug addict's nightmare and we looked, turned the car around, and drove away. I know now that these must have been but very big cows and nothing more, but my memory tells the story of cows as large at least as Babe, Paul Bunyan's blue ox from 1930s Minnesotan folklore.

Those many years ago the same friend and I also found the occasional abandoned house down these forest roads. Surprisingly, these seemed to be family homes built deep in the woods—two-story dwellings often with signs of the family—now lost with the years —years that have simply ridden away on the wind. In one house, children's crayon drawings on papers were still lying about. Another house had a note stuck on a wall—a note that someone had left many years before. As I remember, it stated where the writer had gone and when he or she would return.

There was something very moving and disturbing about such finds—for they portrayed so clearly the passage of time. They starkly showed a bygone era and a family life that once meant everything to someone and that was now forever gone.

Another house stands out across the years in my memory. Inside it, a piano was wedged in the stairway. How many years it had been there was impossible to say. I guessed that the movers had dropped the piano on their way down the stairs and it had become lodged so fast that it was judged broken and immovable and therefore simply abandoned. I remember reaching up and strumming the harp-like array of 88 x 3 strings laid open above me and hearing throughout the house their eerie ringing like the sound of some giant autoharp.

In 2001, however, we saw no abandoned houses. The dirt road we took had signs on it that said, "Loon Song Bed and Breakfast." This road was just a few hundred yards from our usual haunts of the past and yet on it might be something new and different and maybe even mystical. We drove down the road, occasionally stopping to get out with binoculars to mark down a few more birds on our lists. Along the road were more quaint signs about the bed and breakfast and finally, at the end of a turn, we came upon an overlook of the Loonsong.

There was a very large lake below and a breeze wrinkled its dark blue water. Just above the lake was an inn built of wood. One or two cars were parked in back of it. We felt that the Loonsong was a place where rather well-to-do or famous people might stay for a few summer days. The place was private and secluded and very quiet. And it had its own lake. But that was just the impression of a couple of Arizonans. In Minnesota, a private lake is nothing. Even in Itasca Park, fishy Squaw Lake is mostly left alone by anglers and it has lake trout! Fifteen percent of the state is covered with water and fishermen and anyone else have little reason to congregate on the shores any particular lake.

McDonald's Trading Post—A Grassy Field with a Bit of Scraggly Blackberry in It—Left-Wing Country Folk—"You Can Have a Drink. Whatever You Want."—"Those Are the Beatles, I Believe."—A New Dirt Road Expedition—Lost!— The Mystery and the Magic Once Again

We took another dirt road expedition which started at the former site of McDonald's Trading Post. There was nothing left there but a grassy field with a bit of scraggly blackberry in it. The field lay at the dirt crossroads at the edge of the forest. The trading post had burned down and the senior McDonalds had passed away years before. I remember that even in the sixties, they were quite old. They spoke with thick country accents. My father once told me that they were practically run out of the Twin Cities—hardly redneck towns—because they were so radical in their left wing beliefs. I never saw that aspect of them except that they liked my parents and so whenever I went in for a cheeseburger there, they simply refused to let me pay. They reminded me of the characters in The Grapes of Wrath—the character that Henry Fonda played for example—but much older.

Mrs. McDonald once told me, "We don't fly."

To which I said, "Well, how do you travel?"

She said, "We take the train." In her midwestern drawl. "We really like it. You can have a drink. Whatever you want."

These are the only words I remember from her in any detail, but I remember the words exactly. I have but one clear recollection of what her husband once said. We were listening to the juke box in the trading post and he said, "Those are the Beatles, I believe," which was kind of a hip thing for a guy that age to say; the Beatles were quite new. Bill Underhill, a friend of my brothers and sisters and I, said very kindly, "Well, no— actually that's the Dave Clark Five—but they sound like the Beatles sometimes."

"Ah," said Mr. McDonald, seemingly pleased to learn.

Sally and I started a new dirt road expedition at the site of the old McDonald's Trading Post. I drove the rented Alero off to find more magic and mystery and within minutes was completely and totally lost. This wouldn't be a problem if I were with my other sister, but Sally is afflicted with the same malady as I: she has absolutely no sense of direction—at all. NONE.

I drove. I tried one dirt road after another. Finally, I got on a highway. I saw nothing familiar so I found another highway and started driving down it. Time passed and I must have been doing sixty for much of it and I was sure I had left most of Minnesota behind and would soon be in Ontario or maybe North Dakota. All I had tried to do was to find a bit of mystery and magic down a dirt road—the way I had done so long ago—and now, instead, I was hopelessly lost.

Finally, in despair, I got off of the highway and took a lonely dirt road. I drove down it and stopped. There I saw a grassy field with a bit of scraggly blackberry in it. The field lay at the dirt crossroads at the edge of the forest.

I was back at McDonald's.

FIRST GRADE IN 1957

PILLOWS AND NAPS—WE *DASSN'T* WAKE RONNIE!—
BATHROOM DISASTER—A LITTLE NEGRO BOY—
SUNDAY SCHOOL—A LITTLE CART—HULA SKIRTS—
BARE NAKED!—TRADITIONAL FAMILY VALUES

It was nap time in Mrs. Beata's first grade class at Louisville, Kentucky's Audubon School. We all lay our heads on the pillows that our moms had made for us and pretended to sleep. Of course, nap time was a pleasant fiction. We couldn't really sleep sitting as we were at our desks, our bodies bent three ways, but we played the game. Nap time was simply an attempt to get us to wind down and give the teacher a break.

This time, when nap time was over, Mrs. Beata told us all to be very quiet—very very quiet indeed. Ronny, it seemed, had fallen fast asleep during nap time and we *dassn't* wake him up. Waking him up would not be nice. The message was clear: we were nice people and we would never be mean enough to wake someone up—not someone who was fast asleep.

Mrs. Beata continued the class speaking softly so as not to waken Ronny, but all the while she kept a stealthy eye on the boy. She paced the room nonchalantly until finally she let out a colossal, "AHAH!"

"I SAW him!" Mrs. Beata screamed. "He wasn't really asleep. I saw him open one eye just to see where I was!" Mrs. Beata was shaking in fury.

"Look at him! Look at him moving his foot in and out of his shoe!"

I looked, and sure enough, Ronny's heel came up out of his leather shoe once or twice and then stopped. I reckoned that if I had shoes like that I would do the same thing. It looked as though my foot might feel real nice and relaxing lazily sliding in and out that way. I didn't have any shoes like Ronny's; they weren't my style—but I could relate.

Mrs. Beata continued to scream at Ronny, who just kind of shriveled up twitching and crying.

Now, being only six years old, Ronny nor the rest of us had any idea that Mrs. Beata's behavior was out of whack. But this episode passed, and if Mrs. Beata had to answer for it from Ronny's parents, we sure weren't aware of it.

I found that Mrs. Beata hated little girls. There was a bathroom in the classroom and the children all lined up to use it. One day, a little girl standing behind my brother said, "May I go in front of you?" To which, my brother responded, "No, you may not."

The door to the bathroom had a ventilation grate near the floor, and when my brother turned to come out of the bathroom, he saw through that grate a rain of urine. The rest of us got a better view. The urine showered down from her dress and spattered at her feet. The little girl stared at Mrs. Beata with a mixture of the most horrible shame mixed with what was clearly fear. She did not look to her teacher for help or compassion and her instincts were correct; Mrs. Beata reacted with rage. She screamed at the little girl and told her what a horrible person she was. Then she went into the bathroom, got a wad of paper towels, and made the child kneel alone and wipe up all of the piss in front of the entire horrified class. In front of all of us.

Now, being only six years old, none of us had any idea that Mrs. Beata's behavior was out of whack. But this episode passed, and if Mrs. Beata had to answer for it from the little girl's parents, we sure weren't aware of it.

Mrs. Beata told us that there wasn't a Negro within twenty miles of our school. She said that if we did have a little Negro boy in class we would be very nice to him. She also said that they had dumb names like "Ray." We didn't know the real reason we didn't have any little Negro children in our class. It was not because there weren't plenty around in Louisville. It was that the school was segregated.

As if she didn't have enough faults, Mrs. Beata was also religious. I remember how she told us all about Jesus. Perhaps there were no Jewish children there, but she didn't bother to ask. Why should she in 1957? I remember the story she told about how Jesus was called upon to visit the family of a dead little girl. Mrs. Beata told us of how the bereaved mother lifted the little girl's arm and dropped it, and how it fell so limply that there was no question that she was dead. "Well," said Mrs. Beata, "Jesus laid his hands on her and that little girl rose and walked again." She didn't say whether Jesus would have made the little girl wipe up her own piss.

My parents were devout atheists but if Mrs. Beata had to answer to them for proselytizing I sure wasn't aware of it. Every Monday morning the students were asked to tell what they did in Sunday school. Since

154

atheists didn't go to Sunday school, I was left out of this part of the class and I was immediately annoyed at it. One Monday morning, when Mrs. Beata asked what we all had done at Sunday school, I got fed up and I raised my hand.

"Yes, Tommy." said Mrs. Beata.

"My dad says he's gonna build me a little cart!"

"That's very nice," she said. "But it has nothing to do with Sunday school."

"I know," I said.

Mrs. Beata's First Grade Class Hawaiian Show was a big event. All of the little boys got their moms to supply them with flowered shirts, and they made cut-off Levi's with the pant legs clipped as if with giant pinking shears so that teeth-like triangles of fabric formed the cuffs. They looked very Hawaiian that way. We all wore leis too. The girls would be dressed in grass skirts, rustling affairs made of endless strips of crate paper.

In class, a week before the show, the little boy next to me said, "Underneath those skirts, the girls are going to be bare naked!!"

I judged they wouldn't be naked, but from what I gathered it would be possible to see their underwear quite clearly and in the first grade, that was really something. We all looked forward to the Hawaiian Show. We learned some Hawaiian sign language and I was chosen to strum the autoharp. Mrs. Beata, you see, had an autoharp and I proved to be the best at strumming it as she pushed the buttons labeled: "C ... A minor ... F ... G... and so on.

I remember only snippets of the Hawaiian Show, but I remember in detail what happened afterwards . We

155

all returned to our regular classroom, still in our Hawaiian wardrobe. Mrs. Beata looked at all the girls and said, "You girls DO understand, don't you?"

That served as the cue, and immediately, all of the girls exploded into action. Right there in the classroom, they tore their leis off and then their skirts until they were clean down to their underwear and nothing else! And then they dove desperately into their regular school dresses. All of them. Right there in class.

When it was happening I was stupefied with shock. My teeth were clenched. "They're all bare naked!" I said, and the boy next to me replied: "I know, but don't talk about it now!" His face and body were twisted with emotion.

Mrs. Beata could have had the girls take turns changing in the bathroom. Should could have got another teacher to watch the boys in another room. She could have done anything. Instead she chose to make the darkly subconscious and archetypal nightmare of showing up in class in your underwear a reality—a realty! She did that to all of them. Every single one. But if she had to answer to a single one of those little girls' parents I sure as hell didn't hear of it.

I have a feeling that in many ways my 1957 first grade class was closer to the rule than the exception than one might think. And so whenever I hear people longing for traditional family values (with a naive sigh and a maudlin flourish of trumpets) or hear them bitching about having to be PC and missing the good old days when they had the upper hand (with the blacks in the back of the bus and so much more), I think about Mrs. Beata.

THE JOY OF CATALOGS AND MY CASINO GUITAR

HAVAHART TRAPS—RELCO METAL DETECTORS AND
MY TX-60—FISHING LURE SPOONS—COFFEE TABLE
CATALOGS—PIRATE REGALIA—CLIPPER SHIPS AND
SEASCAPES

I have always loved catalogs and I have a small collection of them that are dear to me. My oldest is "Trapping with Humane Havahart Traps." The copyright date on the catalog is 1945, and even I don't date that far back myself—but I figure that I got it in around 1962 because the inside cover reads "Revised 1962" and that date seems about right. My address is written on it in longhand with a real fountain pen. No zip codes back then. The catalog is a small booklet containing very high quality line drawings of animals and some black and white photos. Aside from these, it is mostly a collection of testimonials from satisfied customers. I remember reading it over and over again.

I never bought one of their humane traps.

I also still have my old Relco Company catalog from around 1971. Relco manufactures metal detectors and I spent hours staring at the different models: the Coin-Ranger at $97.50, the Frontiersman at $129.95, and the Pacesetter—was $279.50 now only $198.50! The catalog was also full of user testimonials, some of them hand-written, and I read the catalog for months until I finally broke down and sent away for the TX60, the $69 model. I had a lot of fun with that detector although it didn't function as well as it was advertised to because the catalog would have you believe there were more pieces of eight and doubloons around than there really are. Still, I found a lot of pennies and pop tops. Remember pop tops?

I still have my TX60.

A few years ago I went on a fishing lure kick and started collecting spoons—fishing lure spoons, of course. Lure catalogs range from simple black-and-white booklets to slick brochures with page after page of glossy color photos. Those high quality catalogs always surprised me because I knew they must have cost a fortune to produce and print and while a few companies asked for a dollar to cover expenses, more often than not the catalogs were absolutely free. Even at a buck a throw, I viewed them as slim coffee table books and a tremendous value.

I have catalogs for fossil distributors, bird watcher supplies, electronics, books, music instruction, computer software and hardware, and now—as I look through them—a fantastic one called "Of Ships & Sea." When the heck did I get that? From it, you can order all your pirate regalia: wall decorations, anchors, sextants, barometers, ships in a bottle, and prints of famous seascape paintings. I realize suddenly that I want one of those prints with the big old clipper sailing along and one of the ones with the raging sea crashing against the rocky shore and a couple of gulls whirling above it all. How hokey can you get? It's so lame it's cool.

Having said all of this, I would now like to go into
detail about a current catalog and the current adventure
I am having with it. Not so long ago, a catalog came to
me in the mail entitled "Musician's Friend."

I began to thumb through it and was surprised to
find that you could get a real Fender Telecaster guitar
for 314 bucks—and authorized knock-offs brand new
for $149. Stratocasters too.

Now, I already have a Stratocaster—the classic
solid body rock guitar that everyone on earth has seen a
million times—the one Jimmy Hendrix used. Mine's the
familiar sunburst color, but it isn't a real Fender; I
bought it for 189 dollars in 1981. The purchase was a
wise idea because it opened up opportunities and
experiences for me. If someone said, "Hey, we're gonna
put together a little band for the Halloween party. Have
you got an ax?" I could say, sure, I've got one." "What
kind?" "A Strat." "Cool."

I played it when the house band for the Halloween
party was practicing and one of the guitarists came up
and made a big fuss over it. He couldn't believe the
sound. My brother later joked that it wasn't the guitar;
he didn't think the guy was such a hot player and
thought he was impressed whenever good sound came
out of a guitar because he'd never experienced it before

personally. The next time I saw the guy he had a sunburst Strat just like mine except it was a real one.

Little experiences like that get you to thinking and I began (not for the first or the last time) to wonder how much difference there is in guitars—especially electrics. I have an expensive acoustic guitar and it is noticeably superior to your 250 to 300-dollar ax. The action is far preferred—no contest—but the sound I figure is but 4 to 6 percent better. That's just a wild guess. It's a very hard thing to judge. How much real difference can there reasonably be in this wonderful capitalistic world? A 300-dollar guitar would be absolutely contemptible and virtually unsalable if a 1600-dollar one sounded three times as good. Guitars would just be more expensive instruments. It wouldn't be reasonable to expect someone to buy an instrument that would make him or her sound so poor in comparison to hack players with more expensive equipment.

A 1600-buck guitar doesn't out sound a decent cheapie by a very wide margin. The superiority is there, but it is sometimes subtle. Put brand new strings on any guitar and it will sound fabulous for a day or two. Add to that the fact that the sound also depends on who's playing the guitar. A crummy violin player will make a Stradivarius curdle milk. The same applies to guitarists.

My thoughts about differences in quality among different makes of guitar would become a part of my thinking in the weeks that followed. And these questions about quality would continue to occupy me.

I began to stare at the Musician's Friend catalog and opened it to show pages 54 and 55, which displayed an array of 18 Stratocasters, Telecasters, and two or three other models. As I said, there were Teles for 314 dollars. The ad read: "Choose Midnight Wine (shown) Brown Sunburst (add $35), black, midnight blue, or Arctic white finish. I wanted Midnight Wine—a great name and a great color if the picture was right. I knew that Teles could cost as much as $3000 or more so this seemed like a good deal. Soon, however, I began to fixate on the Fender Toronado, a solid body electric whose shape I soon devoutly believed had been designed in accordance with the order of the very cosmos and the music of the spheres.

My God it was a gorgeous guitar—and the black finish with the tortoise shell pick guard was my favorite. In the ad, there was a big circular insert on the guitar's neck that read: "Guitar Player's Pick!" I showed the ad to my nephew, a professional jazz guitarist, and he said that the Toronado was kind of hip in the Grunge circle as Kurt Corbain used to play one before he offed himself. I used the web to find user reviews and they all loved their Toronados and raved about how they screamed.

These Toronados were bad ass rock guitars, but I am a swing guitarist—or long to be—and this wasn't quite the right ax for that style. Traditionally, jazz and western swing have been played on a hollow arch top guitar with F holes like an old Epiphone or a Gibson Super 400 or L-5. And because of this, it wasn't long before I had rid the specter of the Toronado from my mind and begun to concentrate on page 69—the Epiphone page. I stared at the Epiphone guitars: the Epiphone Dot, the Wildkat, the Alley Kat, the Sheraton, and the Casino. Fine-looking guitboxes all of them, but it was the Casino that began to prey upon my mind. The ad read: "Ever since the Beatles purchased three Casinos back in 1964, these hollow Epi's have taken on a life of their own."

What it means to have a guitar take on a life of its own was lost on me, but I knew I would have an Epiphone Casino or die. It listed for $1049 but Musician's Friend sold it for $599. There was a square drawn over the body of the guitar that read: "BEST BUY!"

I was sold.

I remembered John Lennon playing his Casino and I began to search the web to learn more about the guitar and its Beatles history. It seems McCartney bought a Casino and used it to play the famous lick in Lennon's "Ticket to Ride." (This was news that surprised me as I would have thought that Lennon or Harrison would have played that little guitar bit.) John and George soon had their own Casinos and they used them at the famous Shea Stadium concert and at other gigs. The Sergeant Pepper's album is alive with the sound of this guitar as well. People wrote that Lennon couldn't keep his hands off the Casino and it was his preferred instrument to the sad day he died. The user reviews were also glowing.

Pros: Weight, feel, and Tone tone tone !!!!!!
Cons: Not enough time in the day for playing!
The Bottom Line: This is a seriously fine instrument. Forget the History, try it because it is awesome !

People talked all about the P90 pick-ups that could give you the Beatlesque sound and how you could switch between pick-up and tone settings to turn your Casino from a screaming rock banshee into a blues monster or a jazz machine. All of them were impressed with the craftsmanship and attention to detail.

There were only a couple of minor complaints from users:

Dislikes: The only feature I do not like about this guitar is the pick guard constantly vibrated at an aggravating and very noticeable level when I played the guitar unplugged. Since I have removed the pick guard all the bad vibrations are gone. I assume that this may have been a problem for some time since John Lennon removed the pick guard on his Casino.

It was true that Lennon had taken off his pick guard; just look at the Let it Be album and the rooftop concert. John's playing the Casino, and the white pick guard with the cool Epiphone monogram is gone. I doubt, however, that his vintage American-made Epiphone had a rattly pick guard like the Korean model, which was a budget reissue item rebuilt from scratch.

One player also mentioned an internal buzz that seemed to be part of the hardware inside. It was a minor thing that didn't bother him and that couldn't be heard when the guitar was plugged in. And everyone thought the pick-up selector switch was kind of cheap, but easily replaced for a couple of bucks.

Aside from these minor items, the reviews were raves. I studied more about the Casino and found that it was really a copy of the old high-priced Gibson 330, no longer in production. It's a great deal like the present day Gibson 335, but it is completely hollow while most of the others in the Gibson and Epiphone line have solid blocks of wood within them and are semi-hollow. The Casino is therefore very lightweight in comparison.

I also learned that Epiphone is Gibson's low-end branch company. The Epi's are made in Korea and aren't quite as good—but the word on the street is that they are close enough that spending 1500 bucks more for a Gibson is ridiculous.

The Beatles seemed to have viewed things the same way. Paul's trademark violin-shaped Hoffner bass was a very inexpensive instrument—but it was hollow and very comfortable, and so he used it in nearly every performance. The old Epiphone Casino used to be American-made but it was still the low end of the Gibson Company—and that didn't stop John and George from using them—although Epiphone executives surely didn't just pick Casinos off the shelf and ship them to the Beatles. There wasn't a guitar company in the world that wouldn't have killed their first born to get one of their models into the Beatles' hands, so undoubtedly Epiphone sent them the absolute best they had.

John's first Epiphone was a sunburst, but hoping to improve the sound, he had someone sand it down to its natural wood and give it the slightest coating of shellac. His model also had a black ring around the pick-up switch, and, as I mentioned, the pick guard was removed. At the Epiphone web site, you can find the specs for the new John Lennon Casinos. There are two:

one the sanded down version and the other the original sunburst. For the sanded down version, they got permission from Yoko Ono to go to her apartment in the Dakota and study the very instrument John played in order to get their reproduction exact. They have removed the pick guard and put in a black grommet ring and they're selling it and the original sunburst model as limited editions for $2,995 each. They even have a downloadable software presentation on the John Lennon Casino. But I didn't know anything about this when the Casino bug bit me. All I knew was that the picture and short description in the catalog had convinced me.

I used to pop into the local saloon, have a beer, and read or write. But now I had become obsessed and I would have that beer and just sit there and stare at the Epiphone Casino in the catalog. I read nothing; I just stared. And stared. The bar maid at the Timber Wolf Pub said, "Why don't you just buy that guitar?" And eventually I thought, "Why don't I?" I hadn't bought an electric in 20 years at least and $599 wasn't that much money. My nephew told me not to buy from a catalog. He said the quality could vary a lot and to play one first before I bought it. But when I tried to find a Casino in local stores I came up with nothing—and I knew they wouldn't have the cheap price anyway.

I ORDER A CASINO! STICKERS — SET UP IN THE USA! — A RATTLY EPI! — THE BRIDGE IS A PIECE OF S...! — THE PLYWOOD IS S...! — THE TUNDRA OF ILLINOIS — IT'S F... DEFECTIVE! — I SEND MY EPIPHONE CASINO BACK

Finally, I called Musician's Friend—just to inquire about their views on quality. The guy who answered my call was named "Sky."

"Sixties Parents? God love 'em! My name's Rain Cloud!" I was tempted to say, but I didn't.

Sky told me, "If you don't like it, just send it back in 45 days. For any reason." That sounded unbeatable, so I ordered the Casino. Natural finish, of course! Just like Johnny's.

The guitar came in one night after work. I was surprised at how beautifully made it was. The natural wood showed an exquisite grain and the white binding gave the whole instrument a two-tone, saddle-shoe look with the color of a palomino. The neck was mahogany —darker than the rest of the guitar, but not so dark as not to fit in with the color scheme. And there is no other guitar with a headstock shaped that way—there is something very classical about the look of that headstock as though it might go as well on a cello or viola. The action was great and the parallelogram inlays on the fingerboard were just plain cool. The pick-ups, bridge and time-honored but seldom-seen V-shaped tailpiece blazed with the brightest of gleaming chrome. Oh, for sheer looks this was hard to beat. Very very hard indeed.

On the pick guard was a cool sticker that said, "Limited Lifetime Warranty." I reluctantly removed it. (I hate to take that kind of thing off something brand new. I bought a 1990 Dodge shadow new, and when I finally sold it in the year 2001, most of the sticker was still plastered on the passenger window.)

Also on the back of the Casino's headstock was a sticker that said, "Set up in the USA by #15." In the user materials was a picture of a long-haired blond technician setting up an Epiphone guitar.

My brother and a friend came over and we played some music. They had acoustics and I played my new Casino. Although an electric, its hollow body had enough acoustic properties for it to be played along with the other guitars. I was surprised that it was loud enough to do that. A Strat or a Tele could not be heard at all in such a setting.

My new Casino's strings were super slinkies and they buzzed and didn't stay in tune so I put on some new heavier gauge ones and the guitar kept tune great although it seemed that the strings still buzzed. I had to get rid of that rattling buzz and a friend recommended Jenkins' Guitars. He gave them a call and told me they said, "A Casino? It *has* to be set up."

I took it in.

Now, Randall Jenkins is a very portly fellow and boasts to have set up all of Glen Campbell's guitars and Johnny Cash's and everyone else's famous in the whole world. He took the guitar and diddled with it and started tapping it and said, "This thing is rattling all over the place." He wrote "Rattly Epi" on the work order and said it would cost a hundred bucks to try to get it right. Just "try" he emphasized. But I wasn't worried; from what I'd heard this guy could set-up the crates they came in.

But I got bad news when Randall Jenkins finished. He couldn't get rid of the rattle. "You really tried everything?" I asked him over the phone.

His answer was professional and to the point: "I took the whole fuckin' thing apart. That jack was a piece of garbage and so I shit canned it and put in a new one. And that plywood—that plywood is shit! It's is as cheap as it comes and it's five fucking times thicker than it ought to be. They've carved grooves all under it to make up for the thickness. It's shit. So is the bridge. It's a piece of shit too, but I didn't know if you wanted me to put in a real Gibson one for another hundred bucks. I've laced some rubbery material through the strings beneath it the way some Jazz nuts do when they've got a rattly guitar. You may not like it."

"So my guitar is a lost cause?"

"I didn't say that. You come in and see what you think."

I went in to pick up the guitar and one of the technicians, a guy named Dave, was there. "Is Randall in?" I asked.

"Nah, he's blasted outta here," he replied. "What can I do for you?"

I told him I was the one with the rattly Epi.

"Oh, yeah. Let's plug that baby in!" he said, and got the guitar and flipped on the ever ready Fender amp in the front room. A couple of other guys came over and I played a little and it sounded all right.

"Turn it off and play it," one of them said.

I did and Dave said, "Man, you're too fucking good a player for that guitar." I was both happy and sad to hear this. Happy because these musician types thought I was good—although I always feel I have suckered people when they think I'm a good musician—and sad because they were knocking the guitar. "You know,"

Dave went on, "I've got to learn that swing shit. I'm blasted out with rock."

"The guitar's no good?"

"It's fucking defective, man. Listen to it." He grabbed the guitar away and strummed a C9th. "Shit man, that's no kind of guitar!"

I had to admit that it rattled like hell.

"Just listen to it!" he went on, playing a bunch of complicated rock licks. "I bought a Gibson SG from Musician's Friend a few years ago myself. The prices are great. When my SG came in, I found out that it had been frozen up in the tundra in Illinois. Frozen solid. I sent it back to them and told them it was a piece of shit and they'd better goddamned well send me a good SG or else. The next one came in and the headstock was practically busted clean off. I told them that they sent me another piece of shit and they'd better not do it again. The third one was AWESOME!"

"So you think I ought to send this one back?"

"You're too good a player for this guitar. There's a 95 percent chance that the next one will be perfect. Someone's dropped this thing, or the dumb asses who built it fucked up the laminate. The wood itself is rattling. We took all the hardware off of this guitar and when we tapped it, it still fucking rattled."

One of the other guys said, "We're not knocking the guitar. It's the right kind for the style you want to play. It's just defective."

I got the guitar home and played it and it just rattled too much. You could even hear it when it was plugged in. Unplugged it was far worse. Strum a chord and the guitar crackled with a sustained, echoing rattle like

169

distant thunder. I called Randall Jenkins the next day and said, "Hey, man. This thing still rattles like the devil."

Randall immediately became defensive. "Now, I told you the price and that I might not be able to promise..."

"Yeah, yeah," I said. "Relax; I just want to ask a question. You've already got the bread. I want to know whether you think another model like this—one that doesn't rattle—is worth a damn."

"What do you mean?"

"Well, for starters you were knocking the plywood."

"I wasn't knocking the plywood," he contradicted. "I said the plywood is SHIT! All plywood is shit!"

"Well, that's what I mean—that's knocking it." But I couldn't get very far with him. I knew even the finest Epiphone classic jazz arch tops were made of plywood. They all were. I wanted to know if the Casino was a really bad guitar but he was too far into negativity to communicate what I really wanted to know.

"Oh, another thing," Randall said. "There's something about your guitar that I've never seen. Someone's put a sound post in it."

"What's that?"

"It's a little wooden post that connects the top and the back. I looked at it and it was put in professionally —at the factory. Usually I think they're a good idea— but here I don't know. They're supposed to improve the sound and also to help with any rattling."

I asked whether Musician's Friend was notorious for poor quality.

"You got it from Musician's Friend?" he said. "Good. Send it back."

So I did.

THE ARTSTAR GUITAR AND THE SHERATON—ALL THAT IS GOLD DOES NOT LONG GLITTER—MY FRIEND TRIES TO SWAY ME—GET OUT OF MY DREAM! THE CASINO "BLEM—" IT WAS GOOD ENOUGH FOR JOHNNY SO IT'S GOOD ENOUGH FOR ME—MY REPLACEMENT COMES IN —HANG ONTO YOUR DREAMS!

Shortly afterwards, a friend at work picked up my own Musician's Friend catalog and showed me an Ibañez Artstar guitar somewhat like the Casino. It was Japanese made and its ad boasted the super quality it offered and how it was great for swing. It cost only 69 bucks more. The ad read:

AS120 Artstar Electric Guitar
Product #519435

For the guitarists who insist on uncompromised tone. A full-bodied guitar of flawless workmanship and a broader tonal spectrum than any other semi-hollow body out there. It's perfect for jazz, rockabilly, or country swing. Features an all-maple body, medium frets, beautiful abalone fretboard inlays, a Full Tune II bridge, and 2 Super 58 pickups for a warm sound without feedback.

I'd been through this dilemma before though. In the same catalog, for 30 bucks more than the Casino was the Sheraton II. We looked it up on the web and it was absolutely gorgeous. The pick-ups were gold and so was the rest of the metal hardware. The guitar was a flaming red sunburst with white binding and the inlay on the neck was mother of pearl. The headstock had a intricate and spectacular mother of pearl inlay of branching vines all across it. Man alive! It was nearly impossible to beat the guitar's looks, but when I read the user reviews, everyone said the gold wore off in a matter of hours and some complained that the pick-ups weren't that hot. Still, it was tempting.

My friend at work was urging me to buy the Ibañez Artstar. "You want the Casino even though the Artstar might be higher quality?"

"That's right," I told him, without shame.

A couple of times the next week as my guitar was being shipped back to the distributor, he said, "I guess you've still got time to make up your mind about the Ibañez." He was hoping I'd change my mind and have them ship me the Ibañez as the replacement. But there was little chance of that. I knew that neither the Ibañez nor the Sheraton stood up to the rigorous test that I subjected them to. It was the test of the Catalog Dream. I wanted a Casino and nothing, not even the voice of reason could stand up to my living out that dream. How could I get the Ibañez? Every time I looked at it I would think about the Casino!

"Hey, everybody," I thought. "Don't be trying to save me from ruin. I know you've seen the Casino and now you're bored and would just love to see something new. But you won't have to live with a guitar you don't want. This train is bound for glory! Get aboard or get out of my dream!"

While I waited for my new Casino to come in, I went on the internet to look at the Musician's Friend site and found to my surprise that there was suddenly a lower-priced Casino advertised there. It was only available in the natural finish. It was called the Casino BLEM and it cost ninety dollars less. I clicked the button to read more and found that "BLEM" was short for "blemished" and that "blems" were guitars that people had sent back for one reason or another. The company said they might have tiny scratches or other blemishes, but they guaranteed them to be in otherwise perfect condition. I knew that my pick guard had visible scratches on it when I sent the guitar back; you can't really play the guitar without leaving tiny marks like that.

Sending guitars back seemed to be a very common practice. When you call Musician's Friend, one of the first options you hear in the recorded message is the key for returning an item, so they obviously get a lot of guitars returned. Just the same, I worried whether people were sending back natural finish Casinos by the boxes and crate loads because they were all faulty and rattling like mad. That would explain Epiphone's new advertisement. A couple of days later, however, the Casino BLEM was no longer listed on their page, so perhaps by chance it was the very guitar I returned that they had been reselling and some poor slob had bought it.

The two limited edition John Lennon Casinos remained listed on the site along with the regular Korean model available in Cherry, Ebony, Natural, and Turquoise, the last of which is a very unusual color for a guitar. At the bottom of the Casino page they'd written:

If it was good enough for the Beatles, is it not good enough for you? Order today.

Now who could argue with that?

A week or two went by and I checked on the web and saw that the UPS driver had signed the release himself and dumped my new guitar behind my gate. When I got home there was a very battered and half-open box at my house and I opened it up to find the identical twin of the guitar that I sent back—except, to my relief, it didn't have that awful rattle. If you pressed it, a string would buzz and if you hit a big open E there was a barely detectable, but faintly familiar rattle but only when the pick-up selector switch was in the middle position. I'd put my thumb on the switch and the rattle disappeared. It was hard to hear. Perhaps that rattle was my imagination.

I tapped the top of the guitar and there was an airy ringing sound faint and beautiful like a thousand tiny bells. I identified its source when I plucked the tailpiece. The strings that attached to it made the light and ethereal ringing sound but it could not be heard when the guitar was played. I liked the sound anyway. It was pretty.

I couldn't hear any rattles then, even when the pick-up switch was in the middle position. The fifth and six strings sometimes had the tiniest buzz—but who cared? That could be adjusted if I even thought it was worth the effort. There were a couple of tiny chips on the edge of the pick guard. I figured if I made a couple of strokes with a file—carefully!—they'd disappear.

My friend at work still thought I should have gone for higher quality and a Japanese-made Ibañez, but then I found myself back to my question about how much difference there was between two guitars, one considered slightly lower in quality, the other slightly higher. With electrics, the difference was even less important and if I cared enough I would simply buy them both—or the $2000 Gibson. I had the bread. But there was no alternative for me; have you ever tried buying something different from what you had first envisioned and for years afterwards felt the tiniest tinge of regret each time you saw the purchase and contemplated your compromise and your weakness and how things might have been?

Hang on to your dreams!

> Dreams are the only thing
> 'Kept me goin' so far
> Just dreams and the sound of my guitar!

EPILOGUE

So I had my Casino and after all this rattling business, I found out that it had no sound anyway. I took it to a gig and the guys said, "That guitar is wimpy. Just plug in your acoustic and use that." I did. The Casino sat by the stage as a decoration.

I took it into a local music store where the guitar guys had a listen. "I don't like it," the owner said. He called in their champion guitar player who strummed it a few times. He diddled with the amplifier and finally said.

"No balls."

"What's wrong with it?" I asked.

"It has the worst pickups I've ever heard of. Maybe you can replace them."

I tried the guitar out again and again and I couldn't get any sound. It was like holding a microphone up to the guitar. No sound. No joy.

I could have just put in hum-bucking pickups out of the same catalog instead of the dog eared P-90 single coils, but then the Casino wouldn't look or sound like a Casino.

Online I found that there was a guitar pickup guru who lived up around Vancouver. I emailed him and he replied that the covers on the Korean P-90s were too thick, and it muffled the sound of the strings. He could rebuild the innards, however. I took the pickups off the guitar and mailed them to him, and he rebuilt them and sent them back. The guy in the local music store installed them for me and we tried out the new guitar.

"Now it's doing what it should be doing," he said.

But I was sick of the Casino. My dream had died. A friend of mine had a business on Ebay and she helped me sell the guitar to some guy in Norway. He got a good deal because he got the case too and the super smokin' guru-made pickups.

And I switched to a Variax guitar. It's a modeling guitar with a piezo pickup for each string. There's a computer inside the guitar that tells each string, "You're a string on a Little Jimmy Dickens King of the Flattops Gibson J-200 Jumbo acoustic guitar!" Or it might tell each string to be a Mastertone Banjo string or the string on a Telecaster Thinline. The signal from each string goes into the guitar and is converted from analog to digital. Then the software inside runs the signal through some Al Gore rhythms and changes them so that the guitar will sound like a Rickenbacker twelve-string or a 1959 Stratocaster, or a Martin 0-18 parlor acoustic, or even a Casino! It comes with 28 guitars built in.

You can even create your own Frankenstein guitars with the guitar's software. On your computer screen you'll choose from a Mr. Potato Head style of goodies and say, "All right, I'll use the semi-hollow body guitar and put a lipstick P-90 at the neck angled at 35 degrees and a hum-bucking pickup at the bridge. Let's tune the guitar in DADGAD, put a capo at the second fret, and see what she sounds like. If you like your creation, you download it into your guitar. You can even email the code to a friend so he or she can have that guitar as well.

I loved the thing. I bought three of them.

Only I can't trust them. Due to a manufacturing flaw that the company doesn't like to talk about, they tend to cut out when you play. And a piezo will break in the middle of a song, so you're shy one string. Mine cut out when I was singing in a bar in the dusty little mining town of Superior, Arizona, where the friendly bikers would come up and stuff dollar bills in my shirt pocket as I played. "Buy his CD," one of them urged. "If you don't he might not come back."

My favorite candy apple red Indonesian Variax died, so I had the guts from my Chinese sunburst removed and transplanted into it. Now, I'm down to two Variaxes: the red one and a black Korean-made Variax 600 which I got for cheap and for which I bought a tortoise shell pick guard to replace the factory-issue white one. I don't like Johnny Cash very much, so I have always avoided black guitars, but the black and tortoise shell combination made this quite possibly the most beautiful guitar I have ever seen.

I still play the red and black variaxes, but one day I will have to get out a catalog and find something more sensible and reliable.

BLACK BEAN CASSEROLE, NOODLES, AND HONEY

OKRA AND GUMBO—BATTLESHIP GRAY AND ICKY FISH
—LAWLESSNESS—LOCAL BEER—A ROUGH SALOON
NEXT DOOR—THE HOT CLUB OF NEW ORLEANS—THE
HEAVIEST POUR ON FRENCHMAN STREET—RACHEL'S
MUFFELETTA—A ROUX—CRAWDADS—THE RECIPE—
KATRINA—I WALK THROUGH THE RUINS—HONEY—
PELLAGRA—PLUGGED URETHRA—ADJUSTING THE
RECIPE—BRAZILIAN BEEF—FEEDING THE BIRDS

I brought the recipe for black bean casserole back with me from New Orleans just three months after my dog Noodles died and a couple of weeks before Katrina smashed into the city. I had looked in my journal and found that I hadn't visited my sister Sally there in four years, and so I called and told her I was flying down.

Now, to me, New Orleans is a city of food as much as it is a city of jazz. The young Louisianan in the plane seat next to me said, "Ya'll lookin' forward to gettin' back home?" He was speaking to the people across from us as he and I had got odd, aft-facing seats and were flying backwards with no choice but to stare at these people as we flew and, of course, them at us.

They told him that they were.

"I just want to get some gumbo," he went on.

"Okra is what makes gumbo gumbo, isn't it?" I asked him, for I'd heard that this was so but wasn't really sure and felt I had been afforded here the opportunity find out at last. I knew my niece loved the stuff.

"I don't know what's in it," he said with a smile. "I just like it."

Sally lived in Lakeview, a fairly nice, middle class neighborhood. She had a small house there, which she loved, with a decent back yard, and she lived alone, two of her kids being successfully employed and the other, my niece, away at college.

Now, I was born in the south, and I feel even today that my life really began when we moved west in 1958 to the clean, unspoiled desert of Arizona. So I didn't used to like the fact that my sister and my niece and nephews lived in New Orleans. The city was rife with crime and corruption and despite its culture and rusticity was rather unattractive. The place seemed to have a dreary, hosed-out appearance and what's more, there didn't appear to be an easy escape from it. A fishing trip I took once out on the nearby ocean convinced me that the color "battleship gray" had been invented on the Gulf Coast, and I found that dredging around with an oversized hook in those shallow, oily waters for "reds" was marginally fun as a one-time thing, but not much more. And I wouldn't eat one of those icky fishes if you paid me.

I remember once watching a bunch of workmen trying to direct traffic in New Orleans, and I said to my nephew, "Those idiots are directing cars into each other. Someone's gonna crash. You ought to call the cops."

"They wouldn't come," he told me.

My other nephew, a jazz guitarist, came home late one night from a gig, and a drunk ran a red light and totaled the family car. By the time the cops arrived on the scene, the driver was cold sober.

But it is not just the establishment that has a lawless quality; it is the mindset of the people as well. A high school graduation ceremonies note sent home to my sister read, "A limited amount of beer will be served to the graduates."

There's truly a different culture in New Orleans from anywhere else I've been in America, and as I said, I didn't used to like the idea of their living there. I began to change my mind, however, when I saw the convenience of my sister's neighborhood. The veterinarian was two houses down, next to which was an Irish pub named Parlay's, which was next to a coffee house, which was next to the bank, which was next to the hair cutter's. The supermarket was right across the street. She had endless little pubs within easy striking distance and there was live music in them half of the time. The beer you get in a local saloon in Arizona is what my irreverent sister refers to as "panther piss," but New Orleans has its own signature brew called Abita, and it comes in several styles, one of which is a wonderfully hoppy concoction that is a joy to drink. Such local flavor is missing where I live. There are good brew houses in places like Phoenix, but their offerings are not available in every single pub and restaurant in the city, and po'boy sandwiches stuffed full of shrimp or oysters are not standard fare either, so despite their Mexican restaurants, cities like Phoenix still seem to lack a culinary identity.

Sally didn't go into Parlay's because the joint seemed too rough for her, and in fact about a week before I flew down, somebody stabbed a fellow patron in there and the poor man crawled out and died on "the neutral ground," which is what New Orleaneans call the grassy area that separates the two lanes of any divided roadway. I went in and had a beer, but the pub was no good at all to Sally; I didn't say her neighborhood was perfect—just convenient.

As for my nieces and nephews, it didn't do them any harm to have grown up playing music in the funky coffee houses and bars that one finds everywhere in New Orleans, and the awful Louisianan public schools were a blessing in disguise: it was a foregone conclusion that they would be sent instead to excellent private ones, where all three of them turned into rocket scientists, one going on to Yale, one to the prestigious University of North Texas, and one to Oberlin with a nice scholarship just because they liked the way she sang.

On this visit, I went down to the French Quarter to watch my nephew, Davy, play one of his last gigs in the popular band "the Hot Club of New Orleans." Davy had just got married to a Brazilian girl named Angela, and they lived in his house with their little dog, Linda. I was given the dog to hold in the bar because Angela had to work, and they didn't like to leave the dog in the house alone.

Linda yapped nearly constantly through the show, and I got some sideways glances from the tourists and locals at the bar. I kept saying, "It's the guitar player's dog!" But I don't think anyone heard. Linda, however, wasn't the only distraction. Her barking was drowned out by a Dixieland jazz band that stormed into the bar, bass drum pounding in the lead and trombones and trumpets blaring out the ultimate New Orleans cliché, "When the Saints Come Marching In" at the decibel level of a major earthquake. Davy and the other "Hot Club" musicians just kept playing, and when the marching band left, someone said, "Take it home, babe," and they closed their song as if nothing had happened.

John Coleman, the fiftyish clarinet player, got the microphone and said, "We'll be taking a ten-minute break, ladies and gentlemen. In the meantime, I suggest you sample some of the top shelf liquor in this fine establishment. Crystal will be your bartender. She has the heaviest pour on Frenchman Street, and I know you'll appreciate that when she makes one of those top dollar call drinks taste positively affordable."

Coleman would know. He was a notorious lush. But that wasn't going to get him fired. These jazz bands never work the crowd. Showmanship would be considered gauche in such a venue, and so the rummy clarinet player could sit in his chair completely toasted and sleep while the rest of the band played. When it was time for him to solo, he'd stir, come awake, pick up that licorice stick, and blow it like nothing you ever heard. Drunk or sober, he was simply fabulous.

Now for a year or so, I had been watching Rachel Ray's show "Forty Dollars a Day" in which she is given 40 bucks and visits an interesting city to see how well she can eat on that much money. Well, it just so happened that one of the shows was filmed in New Orleans, and I watched it and had my sister take me to the place where Rachel had eaten something called a muffeletta. A muffeletta is a very large, round salami sandwich with home baked bread and an oil and vinegar, chopped olive dressing. The thing is huge and, therefore, somewhat pricy, and while Rachel had been able to cut a deal with them for the sake of the show and get them to serve her a half a muffeletta at half the price, they insisted that I purchase a whole one. I asked them if I was getting the same sandwich that Rachel Ray bought, and they said rather proudly, "Yes, sir you are."

I bought a beer and was advised by the restaurant that if I wanted to drink it on the street, I had to put it in a brown paper bag, this in order to pull the wool over the eyes of the naive New Orleans police, I supposed. I went out and chomped on the sandwich and drank the beer on the same cement steps by the Mississippi where Rachel had eaten on the TV show. I couldn't finish the muffeletta and winded up lugging it around with me for a few days before it was all gone, and in the end I must admit that I was rather glad to have finally finished it.

One night Sally showed me how to make a roux. She was getting things ready for dinner guests and the roux was in preparation for the crawdad dish she was going to serve. That seemed to be another example of the different culture in the city. I remember once when I was invited to a friend's house for dinner, his mom was quick to say, "Oh, we're having waffles." (You know, just in case I didn't like them.) In New Orleans, however, you don't even think to tell the guests they'll be eating mudbugs on a bed of rice. You just invite them over and don't say a thing. They'll eat the crawdads all right—and cry for more!

The next night she showed me how to make black bean casserole. I liked it, so I had her write up the recipe.

BLACK BEAN CASSEROLE

2 cloves garlic
2 tbs olive oil
1 pound ground turkey
1 16-ounce can tomato sauce
2 heaping teaspoons chili powder
2 heaping teaspoons cumin
1 small can corn drained
1 can black beans drained
1 can green chiles
8 ounces of shredded longhorn cheddar

Cook garlic in oil.
Add the ground turkey and brown it up.
Add tomato sauce.
Mix in chili powder and cumin
Mix in the corn, black beans and green chiles
Cook together fifteen minutes.
Now lay flour tortillas in a casserole dish and then layer in the mixture of meat and then cheese and then tortillas and mixture and tortillas and cheese, until the dish is full.
Bake at 350° covered until bubbly and yummy!
Serve.

Sally's close friend Catherine was kind enough to take both of us to the airport. Sally had decided to visit

Arizona, and she and I flew there together and toured the state for a week or so. Then I drove her to Sky Harbor Airport for the flight back to Louisiana.

On August 27, 2005 she called to wish me happy birthday, and I said, "Hey, there's a huge hurricane headed at you!"

"I know," she said. "I'm leaving now for Baton Rouge. I hate this!"

I watched the news reports and watched the storm smash into the city.

It was a national disaster, and though the country was "at war" even the president of the United States was forced to curtail his five-week vacation to get right to work on it, pausing only to cut a cake and play a guitar so there would be time enough to rush the first bottle of water to the scene in four days flat.

The family got word that Sally had made it to Baton Rouge and Davy had escaped to Mississippi with his guitar, his dog, and his new bride. We couldn't contact them for a couple of weeks because communications were down. Katherine stayed in town because she didn't want to leave all of her cats, and there was no word at all from her for some time. Sally finally learned that gunmen were walking down Katherine's street blowing the locks off the doors, and just when they reached her place, a coast guard helicopter sent down a spotlight and plucked her off of the balcony of her three-story walk-up.

Sally's house was under 8 feet of water for two weeks; Davy's had no water damage.

When the town dried out, I flew back to walk through the ruins of what had once been Sally's house,

186

and she and I drove through the endless miles of ghostly neighborhoods with the unmown lawns, the dead trees, the abandoned cars, and the ever present yellow water lines on the walls of every house.

Afterwards, back in Arizona, I remembered the black bean casserole and started to make it nearly every week. I remembered how my dog Noodles had loved to eat any spicy dish, and so I let another dog, Honey, have some. Honey is my brother's cocker spaniel and when construction started on his new swimming pool, it was decided that Honey would live with me. She liked the black bean casserole and soon refused to eat her dog food, choosing instead to wait me out until I finally gave in and she got the people food. Because of the dog, I had to have the casserole handy every day of the week. She would eat fully half of every batch I made.

Honey was Noodles' nemesis. I once brought Noodles over to my brother's and Honey attacked her. Noodles was a Chihuahua/terrier mix and no match for the much larger and stronger cocker. Noodles withstood the attack pretty well, but did not survive her three-year fight against Cushing's disease and died on April 21, 2005 at the age of 15.

Before Honey came to live with me, she had always been relegated to my brother's back yard summer and winter. Now, with Noodles gone and the summer blazing hot, Honey could squeeze in and out of my house at will through the undersized doggy door and sleep in the house in air-conditioned comfort.

The black bean casserole called for flour tortillas, but I am fond of corn tortillas. I have heard that the mixture of corn and beans produces a very strong protein, and this is perhaps the reason why tamale pie and other bean dishes taste so good with cornbread and why succotash is a popular dish. Sometimes the taste buds automatically recognize the taste of nutrition. I remember studying the Hopi Indians and learning how they put ashes in their cornmeal before cooking it. The alkali ashes allow the body to absorb vitamin B and prevent pellagra, but the Hopis who invented this recipe didn't know that—they just knew that it tasted better that way. When my brother mentioned that Honey liked corn chips, I had still another reason to replace the flour tortillas with corn ones. I also doubled the amount of canned corn and used ground beef because I felt the flavor of turkey didn't stand up to the cumin and chili very well.

It began to become a hassle to prepare the casserole so often, and so I tried to wean Honey back to dog food. I would take pupperoni dog treats and stick them into the dog food like sweet waffle cones in some doggy parfait. It didn't work very well. She ate the pupperoni but held out for the casserole.

I worried a little that Honey's diet was getting unhealthy. I knew that once I had taken to feeding Noodles jerky treats every day and one night she couldn't urinate because a bladder stone was lodged in her urethra—a stone I later learned might have been formed by the high ash content of the treats. It was a Sunday night and the vet down the road wasn't available and Noodles suffered all night at the brink of getting toxic peritonitis until I brought her into the vet's and she passed the stone on the floor in a pool of urine and relief.

The vet said that Noodles would have to eat Science Diet for the rest of her life. I tried that for a while, and Noodles didn't like it much, so it wasn't long before I put her back on regular dog food—but with no treats at all.

I took other liberties with Sally's recipe. I began to tire of baking the casserole when all I really had to do was put it in the dish hot, and the cheese that I layered in would melt just as well as it would in the oven. I also gave up layering the tortillas. It was easier to cut the torts into triangles and stir them in. As the dish sat, the tortillas would float in the mixture to find a kind of horizontal equilibrium on their own, and when you cut a slice of the casserole, the cross section revealed a neat stratification.

There were two other changes. The cumin and chili powder obliterated the taste of even the garlic, so I left both the garlic and the green chiles out of the recipe. I told Sally, and she said that if only for the extra nutrition I should leave those things in, but I was skeptical. In addition, I didn't want to bother to brown up the ground beef. I wanted a time-saving alternative to having to cook the beef, and I knew of an easy solution: I could get a can of pre-cooked Brazilian parboiled beef and use that. The Brazilian beef, however, presented a problem that was very real to me.

A little more than a year before, I took Noodles in for a check-up, and the vet noticed that she had gained weight. I had switched to Mighty Dog, which Noodles liked better than other brands of dog food. The vet told me to put her on Science Diet and she would live longer. Reluctantly I did, and Noodles hated it. In a couple of weeks she wouldn't eat at all, so I brought her her favorite food: Brazilian parboiled beef. She wouldn't touch it. Noodles was having kidney failure brought on by Cushing's disease and lack of appetite was its tell-tale symptom.

The vet embarked on a treatment of dialysis that involved a saline drip that was designed to cleanse the blood through the kidneys by the sheer attrition of constant, unremitting hydration. Noodles stayed in a cage at the vet's with an IV for three terrible days, and on the third, I was directed to bring Noodles' favorite food to see if she was better and would eat it. When I arrived, I found her in an absolutely ghastly condition and knew that she would never eat again. After we put her to sleep, I buried her in the back yard and threw the can of beef in the trash.

It took more than a year for me to finally use Brazilian beef again, but I finally added it to the recipe. Honey loved it, and I found that I was able to eat it too, but still not without a pang brought on by the memory of how Noodles died.

On the morning after I added the Brazilian beef to the casserole, I went out into the desert back yard and got the pooper scooper. There in the yard, I saw Honey's stool stuffed fat with the extra corn I had put in the recipe, and it brought to mind the time I had seen Noodles' stool similarly filled with the milo maize which I had left out on the lawn for the Inca doves back before the desert landscaping when the yard was cool and green with grass. And I couldn't help but remember how I had thought the milo might do her harm and how for years afterwards I had given up feeding the birds.

DASH INN

Dash Inn was the only restaurant I ever gave a damn about and I still mourn its passing. The place got its name from its owners Hash and Dee Nelson, who combined their first names to come up with "Dash" and then added "Inn."

Dash Inn was a local favorite restaurant in Tempe for better than twenty-five years. Everyone who was anybody went there.

There were a number of reasons why Dash Inn had a loyal following. For one thing, it was right next to the campus, so it got a solid college clientele. But its locale was hardly the only reason for its success. In fact, the location was a loser for most other restaurants. Right across the street was a swath of land that had served as home to a number of different eateries, every one of which went bust in very short order. And even the franchise "Hobo Joe's" next door, seemed slow to dead while Dash Inn was simply jumping with action twenty feet away.

Dash Inn was a hip joint, and you could see that just by walking in. Hash didn't give long-haired waiters a hard time when they applied for work; he hired them and just made them wear a pony tail the way the waitresses did. This gave the personnel and restaurant a look that attracted the counter culture while its traditional Mexican restaurant format brought in everyone else. Dash Inn's ambiance was definitely a key factor in its success, and so was its food.

Nobody frequents a place just for the vibes; Dash Inn had a number of dishes that kept people coming back. The restaurant's slogan: "Not Fancy; Just Good" described them perfectly. Many of the items on the menu revolved around a salty and spicy ground beef that went in the tacos and burros and enchiladas. The cooks came in to prep at 8:00 AM every day to get that oily meat ready for the steam cabinets from which it would be dolloped out, and, of course, to prep the enchiladas and all the rest of the food that needed to be made ready.

The enchilada sauce was a miracle. At first taste, it seemed vulgar and poorly conceived in the culinary sense. But if you ate an enchilada-style beef burro, you'd be tasting that sauce for the rest of the day in an eructive series of pleasures that let you know that you'd be back again—soon.

The green burro was much the same. Smooth and savory, it grew on your mind the next day and made you want another—the way you watch a movie like Amadeus, say "Eh, well maybe," and the next day just have to see it again. I always fancied I could detect in the green burro a hint of cinnamon, which I didn't otherwise much like and which wasn't in the recipe. Perhaps it was the slightly toasted area of the flour tortilla that made it smell that way. In any case, the flavor of the green burro was so delicate that I never ordered one enchilada style, although lots of other people did.

The guacamole was described by my brother as "creamed grass clippings," a portrayal that sounds depreciative, but wasn't meant that way. Indeed, his words describe the perfect guacamole: what should guac be, after all, but cool and green, and creamy with the flavor of your family memories steeped in the scent of Bermuda grass? Yes, people came to Dash Inn just for the guac the way the musically deaf bought *Rubber Soul* just for the one song "Run for Your Life."

One of the finest culinary creations of all time was the Dash Inn Mexican pizza. It was nothing more than a corn tostado shell with that ground meat piled on it and topped with grated longhorn. It was heated in the oven and garnished with diced tomatoes and canned green Anaheims. The Mexican pizza and the green burro turned casual diners into regulars.

I was, and still am today, an aficionado of the hot sauce made for the table in Mexican restaurants. I don't care much for the salsa-type sauces, the cold squashed tomato stuff with some chopped onion and a sprinkle of cilantro—you know, the sauces they serve up at a tooth-cracking temperature in a metate-like bowl made of fake black basalt. They're cold and stale and, frankly, I'm always afraid they're being recycled to other customers after you leave. Those ingredients ain't cheap, after all. The good table sauces are the ones in the squirt bottle. They're creatively spiced with anything from oregano to winter savory, and they're often cooked, so they will suddenly "turn" and become real sauce. Sure, sure, they get recycled, but they're safe in the sanitary bottle and no one is going to be dipping their chips and greasy fingers into them and re-dipping and slobbering in the bottle or dropping in cigarette ashes. I don't eat anything that I know has been lying out in the open where every bum who walks by can breathe his cigar smoke and halitosis on it. The table sauce at Dash Inn was the good kind, and in addition it was unquestionably the perfect match for the rest of the cuisine. Hash didn't even fool with making any of that cold, unsanitary salsa at all. He knew what was what.

Dash Inn became a way of life. After my family completed any fun activity, the next destination was Dash Inn. Often we went bird watching before going there. We would drive to Headlight Pond or the Verde River and bird until early afternoon. Then we would toast our adventure over a pitcher of beer and the food at Dash Inn. That dining would end the day's productivity as everyone would fall asleep when we got home at around 3:00 PM.

For years, going to Dash Inn was the source of great happiness for everyone I knew. You could relax there and have fun. You knew the waitresses. The place had a beer and wine license. You could run into people there. It was as though you lived in a New York borough where everyone knew everyone else, and there was a sense of community.

In 1973, I graduated from college unskilled and with no ideas for the future. I returned to Tempe, got up my courage, and asked a waitress if she could put in a good word for me with Hash. I felt great when I saw how happy she seemed to be. She rushed over and talked to him, and I had a job—just as a dishwasher—but I was in and officially a part of it all.

I worked from 8:00 to 5:00 and at the end of the second week Andy, the manager came up and gave me my check. He said, "You'll see I gave you $1.65 an hour instead of just $1.60 because you didn't goof off." That was $13.20 a day. I discussed the pay with the guys in the kitchen and we all concluded that it wasn't much, but you could live on it.

Business was good. I once overheard Hash saying, I thought it was slow last night, but we brought in $300.

Dash Inn didn't open until 11:00 AM, so at 8:00 I had no dishes to wash. Thus, I did prep work before the customers came. One job was grating the cheese. There was a back room with a big steel cheese grater and I had to stuff chunks of longhorn cheddar into it and fill white plastic buckets. The work had absolutely no entertainment value. I had to cut up the tortillas for the chips as well.

I worked with Mamacita, the main daytime cook. Her real name was Hortencia Ferdugo. She had been there forever and told me that she had to go home and cook for her "sans" after she finished at Dash Inn. Everyone loved her. One waiter told me that Mamacita told him she only read the National Inquirer because "The other newspapers do not tell you the truth."

She helped me with my Spanish and would always say, "No me molestes, mosquito." if she were annoyed with me. It was a line from a Mexican song. I remember her saying to me once, "I tell you Tomás, this Dash Inn. Year after year. It's the same goddamn shit." It's funny how after 34 years I'm am sure that this is a direct quote. She also once said these exact words: "You all need a place where you can drink and smoke and cuss."

That place was the unused apartment that was attached to the back of the building. I thought it was strange that the nice apartment lay unoccupied back there. When I climbed the ladder and became a waiter, I was glad after a hard night to be able to have a place to drink with the waitresses and waiters.

There were other characters there that I remember with the same recollection of conversation as clear as if the words had been spoken yesterday. One guy was a blond shag-cut cook named Doug. He was skinny and his legs seemed somewhat misaligned as though he had had polio. He was also a drummer in a local band. I asked him if he ever ate the food and he said, "No, I don't eat this dog food," as he covered an enchilada with sauce on a plate that he put in the oven. He slammed the oven door. "It's shit."

He often liked to say, "I'll make someone a good husband—or a good wife." He made a lot of gay references because he was what people would later call a flamer. Curiously, he suddenly married one of the waitresses, a rather rough around the edges broad who always had a cigarette going. It wasn't long before he was confiding in me, "Tom, the other day she says to me, 'I want to go out with other guys!' I say, 'Honey, we're *married.*' So she brings this clown home..."

His wry, sour way of telling stories was really funny.

Lloyd Thomas was the one I saw consoling him when she ran off with another man.

"As far as I'm concerned, we're divorced!" Doug complained.

"Well, relax. Stay cool. Drink your beer..." said Lloyd.

I remember more of Lloyd's words. He was crazy about big Russian novels. Someone came by and gave him a hardback by Someski about a foot thick, and he said, "Oh, thank you! This is going to be *suuuuuch* a pleasure." I make fun, but I rather admired him for reading such big books.

Once when I told him I had written a science fiction novel, he replied in the most softly pensive and serious way, "I tried to write a novel once. But I had to stop. I found... I found that it interfered with...with the ... the poetic techniques that I've developed... over the years."

My brother was there when he said this, and we both agreed that on this one he was pretty much full of it.

My good friend Brian became a waiter as I did and when he came on, he met Donna, a tall, dark-haired waitress that he instantly fell head over heels for. I was kicking myself for not foreseeing this. I asked myself why I hadn't told him beforehand that he was going to meet this terrific girl as though anyone could foretell who would fall for whom. She was all right and a bit of a free spirit. I went to her house, and I remember that there was a huge picture of her topless above the piano. I think it was a piano. It was just an artsy photo. Nothing dirty, though it seemed a bit bold to me.

I look back on my thinking then and wonder about myself. Why would I have imagined that I could foretell my friend's attraction to her—especially when I knew full well that he didn't even like girls? Or did I really even know that? Naiveté. That was what defined me at the time and when I think of Dash Inn, that's what I often remember.

Years before, when Goldfinger was released, the producers were able to have a character named Pussy Galore not because the times were modern or that mores were changing, but because of naiveté. People would hear the name and say, "Well, come on. They can't mean *that!*" That's how they got away with it.

Such was my naiveté. When I quit Dash Inn, I had saved a ton of money and went to Europe. I remember walking in a red light district of Munich and seeing these painted ladies in windows along the street. I said to myself, "Jesus Christ, what slutty-looking women. If I didn't know better, I would swear they were prostitutes!"

How could this be? I was a latch key kid. My parents were quite worldly atheists at a time when just saying the word would get you fired. My mother was special kind of rebel, a no-nonsense former WWII fighter pilot in the WASPS, who had absolutely no hang-ups. She had a wonderfully tolerant and progressive viewpoint and her politics were slightly to the left of Leon Trotsky. She wanted to make sure that I was never frustrated or inhibited. We were unconventional, and quite wholesome, mostly. Just the same, while other teenagers worried about sneaking girls into the house, I was encouraged to do so. I had no rules imposed on me, I hung out with the wilder crowd, and was the object of what my sisters now call benign neglect. So how could I have been so unstreetwise?

We had a company party at Dash Inn, which was really happily anticipated because we got to close the restaurant and had the whole place to ourselves. Brian had had a falling out with Donna, and there was a dishwasher about our age named Carlos. He was a Yaqui.

The Dash Inn party took up most of the afternoon. When it was time to leave, I went into the kitchen to get Brian and found him smooching with Carlos.

"Let's go," I said.

Brian tore himself away from Carlos, and we walked back to my house, where my mother asked Brian, "Well, was the party happy and gay?"

Brian smiled and said exuberantly, "It was both happy AND gay!"

I wasn't just naive about my friend's sexual orientation. I was naive about everything. Take the plastic buckets in the restaurant. I was naive about them too. I studied the system of food preparation at Dash Inn and noticed that it revolved around the use of these buckets. Some had holes cut in them and were used as colanders and set inside other buckets that caught the water that drained from the washed lettuce. Others were used for multi-gallon batches of hot sauce and still others to store the unfinished food in the refrigerator for the next day. I had a keen eye for business practicality and prudent practices. I felt that such dependence on these buckets was unwise. What if something happened to the buckets? A theft. A fire. What would you do then? It would take you forever to scare up a new set of these buckets. Obviously they had once been used to hold lard or some other product. How long would it take you to use up enough lard to have a complete set of buckets again? Answer me that! Oh, they were living right on the edge with this ill-advised bucket dependency. By God, the fools had put the whole goddamned business at risk. It never occurred to me that such buckets might be manufactured and sold separately—without any lard in them at all. It never crossed my mind that whenever he felt like it, Hash could drive down to some depot somewhere and buy as many of these stupid buckets as he wanted.

Naive? I could tell you stories!

When I was a child, my sisters must have known what a sucker I was. They told me of a magical place where I was going to go. It was filled with extraordinary marvels and all kinds of wondrous things to see and do. "AND," they said, "The FISH jump up and give you balloons!" I couldn't wait. They didn't tell me I was going to the dentist or that the dentist's name was Pat LeDan and that he didn't have any Novocain and that the sound of his drill alone could make people rise clean out of the chair and that he drilled holes to fill imaginary cavities in your baby teeth. I had to get into that dentist's chair on numerous occasions afterwards—but only after the adults were able to pry me out from under the table in the waiting room.

Yet even after Pat LeDan, I remained naive.

My father and I went to Dash Inn sometime in the mid seventies, and Hash greeted us. He said, "I'm opening a new restaurant in Glendale. It's called ¿Qué Pasa?" He got out a piece of paper and wrote on it, "Dinner for Two" and signed it "Hash Nelson." My dad put it in his wallet, but we never drove out there. Glendale was much too far away.

The years passed, and Hash sold the restaurant, but the place kept the same recipes. Lloyd Thomas and some of the others I knew worked there for a decade more.

One day I went in and found that the place had changed owners again and that the bastards had scrapped the menu. I was enraged. "We have a pretty respectable taco," the waiter told me. I gave him a ferocious glare. I hated him, and I got up and stormed out in a snit. I never came back. Later the university got its talons on the property and they bulldozed the building.

***

Twenty-five years passed, and I often thought of the restaurant in Glendale. I constantly longed for Dash Inn food and finally one day, it came to me on a flaming pie that it might just be possible to drive over there and eat. It was a crazy idea, but I somehow I thought it just might work.

I got up one Saturday morning in 2000 and drove all of the way to Glendale to dine at ¿Qué Pasa?, and I loved the place. They had a more polished steel look than the old Dash Inn, but the decor was unlike any other place: there was lavender everywhere and the furniture had a sturdy fifties retro shape and form that I had seen nowhere else. The dark ceiling was covered with tiny lights to give the impression of being under the stars. I swear they had the same beat-up white porcelain plates. And the food was exactly the same. The only casualty was the creamed lawn clippings. I grieved for the departed guacamole, but I was grateful for the miracle that the rest of the entrees yet lived.

A couple of years later, I was attending a conference at AGSIM, the American Graduate School of International Management. It was right next to ¿Qué Pasa?, so I got my co-workers to come with me for lunch there.

Only we couldn't find it. It was gone. The building was empty. We wound up eating at some lousy chicken place.

***

I spend time occasionally now googling Dash Inn and ¿Qué Pasa? hoping to find that someone has opened a restaurant to bring those magical dishes back to life. But all I find is the defunct phone number of the Glendale restaurant and a reference made by some other old-time diner who speaks of Dash Inn in his blog. I emailed him and he didn't do a careful job of reading apparently, for he quoted me as saying, "A cyber friend tells me that Hash is still doing great and runs a restaurant to this day in Glendale with the same tasty dishes!"

I ignore his error and google Dash Inn. Defunct 20 years, the restaurant has more than 1,800 Facebook fans.

SHEARWATER JOURNEY

AUK—PELAGIC TRIP—DEBRA SHEARWATER—ARTHUR
SINGER—THE SHORT-TAILED SHEARWATER—"MUTTON
BIRDS"—$185 FOR A DAY-LONG SEA JAUNT—"A CRAPPY
HOTEL IN A BAD NEIGHBORHOOD"—THE GLASS BEACH—
PATCHES OF BLACKBERRIES—CRUMBLING CLIFFS—A
FAMILIAR BREWERY—BLUE HERRINGS—LIGHTHOUSE—A
GRAVEYARD—A BUM HAVING FUN WITH A BOTTLE AND A
GUN—UNCLE DONNY POPS—BLUE WHALE—CHUMMING
WITH POP CORN—AUKLETS, JAEGERS, SHEARWATERS AND
ALBATROSSES—A BABY COWBIRD BITES ME!—FOLLOW
THAT BIRD!—A SALMON SHARK—THE COWBIRD HEADS
FOR HOME

This is a story about a sea birding adventure and a minor but surprising rescue at sea. I went aboard the ship, the Trek II in Fort Bragg, California because I had always been interested in the pelagic birds, the ones that spend their lives soaring over the open seas hundreds or even thousands of miles from land.

If you're a crossword puzzler, you know that the cue "seabird" calls for the word, "auk" and the auks and their allies—murres, puffins, auklets, murrelets, guillemots, and dovekies—are one major group you are looking for if you go on a pelagic trip. I had never seen a single one of these birds, nor had I ever seen any of the tubenoses: shearwaters, fulmars, albatrosses, storm petrels, etc., so years ago, I asked a friend how one went about seeing any of these pelagics. He told me to call up Debra Shearwater.

"Who?" I asked.

"Debbie Shearwater," he answered. "She organizes pelagic bird watching trips off the coast of Monterey."

"Shearwater?"

"Well, obviously she wasn't born with that name; she changed it."

I called up Debbie and none of her trips fit my schedule.

Well, way led onto way, and I didn't get around to calling her back for several years. A coworker last year set me back on track when she gave me a book called Water and Marsh Birds of the World. It was illustrated by the great Arthur Singer, and I started to read it. The short-tailed shearwater caught my imagination as I read. The short-tailed is a pelagic species that, true to the name, visits *terra firma* only to breed. Like the other pelagics, the bird spends its life flying across the vast, open ocean far from the sight of land.

The short-tailed shearwater builds a deep burrow to lay its eggs on the islands between Australia proper and Tasmania, and when it has finished its reproductive duty, it takes once more to sea, flying up to New Zealand and then clockwise all the way along the thousands of miles of western Pacific, past Korea and Japan, over the Bering Straits, and down the coast of California. Then, somewhere well off of the coast of southern Baja, its path leads it outward, over thousands of miles of open sea—half a world of water towards home.

The mature shearwaters may find their efforts to breed on the islands somewhat disappointing; the Australians harvest the young shearwaters from their burrows and sell them canned as "Tasmania Squab" or

"Mutton Birds." They are considered a delicacy. This at first would seem to present some concerns. There are, after all, too many endangered birds already, and some like the long-billed dowitcher are only with us now because market gunning has been outlawed by governments. Happily, Australia regulates the shearwater harvest now, and though hundreds of thousands of "squabs" are wrested from their burrows and butchered, the species still flies in enormous numbers over the Pacific.

The fascinating facts about the short-billed shearwater got me thinking about Debbie Shearwater and her sea birding trips, and I booked a $185 day-long jaunt on a ship in Fort Bragg, California.

I travelocitied everything, but I made one mistake when I booked a room in the Fort Bragg Travelodge; I checked its user reviews too late. One read, "A crappy hotel in a bad neighborhood." Another, "Don't stay here unless you're a real budget traveler! I was seriously scared in my room." Still another, "Not clean, not safe, actually scary."

"Gosh," I thought. "Two of them mentioned safety, and one talked of meth addicts hanging around. This lodge is not for me."

I'm the kind of guy that meth addicts bother. Junkies too. For some reason, they see me as an easy mark. I rebooked, talking the nice Asian Indian telephone staffers at travelocity into waiving the $25 cancellation penalty. It was, after all, a matter of life and death.

My new lodgings were at the Glass Beach Bed and Breakfast at a good savings. I telephoned and told them about my Travelodge fears, and they in turn sympathized but neglected to tell me that they were exactly—I mean directly—across the street from the lodge and that the deadbolt lock on my cottage was broken. But I didn't mind because it was such a nice place, and I got free breakfast.

My host and hostess told me that their B&B was called the Glass Beach because the ocean used to be used as a dump and all of the millions of bottles in the trash got sanded and polished and now washed up on the beach for people to collect. Before my trip ended, I made sure to spend some time finding the prettiest of these nature-made cabochons: clear, coke bottle, beer bottle, and green. I'd done much the same thing thirty-seven summers before at Moonstone Beach in Rhode Island, where stones washed up perfectly shaped for rings or bolo slides. I never was lucky enough to find a real moonstone, though. But I have kept what I found for all of these years. And I'll keep my Glass Beach stones as well.

The Glass Beach itself was only five minutes from the B&B, and I walked there, getting a good look at the Travelodge. It didn't seem so bad. I went past a lumberyard and found a dusty path between giant patches of blackberries. Many of the berries were ripe. Along the path were also ice plants—those big stalked kind with the blades looking like dill pickle spears. A few families with kids were on the path and down on the edge of the ocean. The beach was surrounded by crumbling bluffs and rocky cliffs. The water was filled with floating seaweed, long yellow-brown tubes as big around as your arm with bulbous, frilled ends. The air had a disagreeable smell. Some blackbirds were flying in and out of some brush offshore, and I hurried over in the hopes that they might be tri-colored blackbirds, but no luck; they were the garden variety red-winged kind.

Back near the shore, I raised my binoculars and saw a fairly large bird with white wing patches. It seemed a weak flyer as it struggled to get over the water to the cliffs. Its feet were bright red. "That's a pigeon guillemot!" I said to myself in surprise. I was pleased at first because I had always wanted to see one. I was also a little disappointed. The pictures in my field guides led me to believe that this was a true pelagic, never near shore. A lot of the romance I'd built up surrounding this species faded when I saw it puddling around in the water like a common mud hen. But it was still a great bird to get on my list.

On the rocks nearby was a group of black turnstones. Funny; they were far and away more pigeon-like than the guillemot, as is the ruddy turnstone, which I see at the family beach house on the Sea of Cortez. The black turnstone isn't present there, nor is the black oyster catcher, which I would see flying by in the distance a little while later.

A giant western gull was flying towards shore with a long ribbon of seaweed in its bill. Was it just showing off? No, it landed on a rock, and I could see that there was a crab tangled up in the seaweed. The gull started tearing off the crab's legs and flinging them down its throat whole. A black turnstone waddled up to see if there might be anything left for him.

I was happy to get two more life listers at the beach, Brandt's cormorant and the pelagic cormorant, and then

I was ready to go back to my room. It had already been a long day. I'd taken a jet from Phoenix to Sacramento and driven for hours on the long, twisting two-lane roads to Fort Bragg. I had the whole next day free, so I would have plenty of time to explore the beach some more later.

I remembered that when I drove into town, I saw a brewery, and it was just three blocks from the Glass Beach Bed and Breakfast. My inner compass unerringly led me there.

To my surprise, I had heard of the place. It was the North Coast Brewing Company. They make Seal Ale, which is for sale in my local Sunflower Market. I took my place at the bar. Through the window across the street, I could see the actual brewery, a separate building.

The bar sold nothing but their homemade stuff. No Miller Lite® or anything else like it. Good for them, I thought. I got an India Pale Ale and chatted with some tourists who were drinking Old Rasputin, a Russian imperial stout. One of the guys had lived in Phoenix as a child. The barmaid was a native of Fort Bragg. Born there. An American guy and his German girlfriend wanted to talk about birds after they saw my bird book. They had many misconceptions. You know the kind: that birds are ubiquitous except for maybe the ostrich, that they migrate by flying at 40,000 feet and riding the jet stream, and so on. I always try to straighten people out on the basics.

"No, no," I said. "You probably didn't see a crane. We've only got two, the whooping crane and the sandhill crane, and neither was a likely sighting for you. You probably saw a heron, a great blue heron."

I had a feeling of satisfaction because later, I knew, they would be passing on this new knowledge and would say to a friend, "No, no! That isn't a crane. It's a blue herring!"

The brewery served pricy food on white tablecloths, so I went and ate at a Mexican restaurant.

The next morning, I drove around the area. There was a nature walk down to a working lighthouse near the town of Casper, and I took it. Along the trail, I found a noisy little flock of bushtits and a few chestnut-backed chickadees. I'd seen the bushtit five times before but the chickadee only once, in Vancouver. Down towards the lighthouse, you could look at the sea over crumbling cliffs. A sign read: "DO NOT APPROACH THE CLIFF," and it had a drawing of a child in shorts who had stepped too close and had caused the rocky edge to break away and fall, taking him with it.

A little later, I pulled my rental car off the side of a road and walked up a path up to a graveyard. All along the trail in the redwood branches, chestnut-backed chickadees hopped and snicked, and I quickly grew tired of them. An *Epidonax* flycatcher hopped down to the ground and then flew back up into a redwood tree.

The graveyard had a sign asking people to be respectful and not to desecrate the graves. Fair enough. I walked through the graveyard and looked at who died and how long they lived and whom they were buried with. One grave marker was made of welded steel in the form of an anchor. It was spray painted green. Obviously, the person buried there had made his living on the sea. He was born in 1941 and died in 2002. Sixty-one years old.

I did not desecrate any of the graves.

I visited a few of the beaches. All of them were bordered by water so full of seaweed that you would have trouble swimming through it without getting tangled and drowned. I didn't know that not far from Fort Bragg was a canyon where you could see wrentits, unusual little birds with funny faces and an odd shape. I would have gone there had I known, but I went back to my room instead, parked the car, and walked down to the Glass Beach and collected glass gemstones. I saw a wandering tattler on some rocks, and later I saw a birder walking down to the beach. I knew she was a birder because she had roof prism binoculars. Hardly anyone but birders buy that kind. She was doing a survey of the beach for the Audubon Society. I told her about the wandering tattler and she said that such a sighting was a big deal and went off to find the bird.

I'd eaten up the day driving around. I had seen few birds, but the real idea of this free day was to make sure I wasn't rushed and could ease into the boat trip the following morning. I judged after a time that another visit to the brew house was due, and I walked back to my room. On the way, I ran into a drunken street person. He said, "How's it going bro?"

"Great!" I told him. He was drinking beer out of a quart bottle. On his hip was a long barreled pistol in a red leather holster. He seemed to be trying to hide the gun under his untucked shirt. I was glad he hadn't asked for money because I don't like to disappoint gun-toting rum-dumbs. I thought of asking him if he was staying at the Travelodge but thought better of it.

About forty-five minutes later, I started off from my room on the way to the brewery. Then I stopped. There was the drunk not a block away sitting on the side of the road. A young guy walked by and the drunk got up and shook his hand. "Damn," I thought. "He sure hasn't gone far." I walked across the street to avoid him, went the three blocks, and then crossed the street again to the brewery. I drank two India Pale Ales.

I decided to walk around a bit and find a cheaper place to eat. I ran into the drunk again. Over by the Welcome Inn, he had the holster off his belt and was doing something or other to it. I said to myself, "Are there, like, police in this burg?"

Not all of the people were bums. The town folk were everywhere walking. There were some young people, but most of the folks out and about seemed at least fifty, beards and pony tails on many of the men. Everyone looked a little wind blown. One family walked by, and a woman said, "Thank you so much, Uncle Donny! We'll get it next time."

Uncle Donny must have popped.

Fort Bragg isn't a bad place. A little run down, but not bad.

I ate at the Mexican restaurant again.

I arrived at the wharf an hour early the next morning. I didn't want to miss the boat by finding out too late that California had a different time zone or something. I knew darned well what time it was, but my compulsive nature would not allow me to tempt fate by arriving on time instead of way early.

In a while, Debbie Shearwater showed up and asked for ten bucks extra for some fuel tax. Twenty-five others arrived a little later, and after a ten-minute talk on boat etiquette, safety, seasickness pills, and birds, we disembarked.

Five of the people aboard were leaders and experts at identifying seabirds and other sea creatures. We hadn't even got beyond the sight of land when one of them started screaming.

"Blue whale!" he shouted. He neglected to say, "Off the stern!" or "At six o'clock!" as we were all told to do.

Seeing a blue whale, the largest animal that ever lived, was quite a big deal to everyone. We chased it with the boat. We'd stop and wait to hear the animal breathe. It was a huge sound, and you could see the column of spray out of its blow hole. The hump that I saw did, indeed, look blue. The whale would disappear, and then we'd see it rather far away. This made us think that we may have been looking at two of them.

After a while, we stopped chasing the whale as it was going in the wrong direction. The boat headed out to sea and we soon lost sight of land. Debbie Shearwater had brought a huge bag of popcorn which she explained would be used as chum. I wondered how long it would last, but I needn't have worried. One of the leaders would stand at the stern and every few seconds drop a single kernel into the boiling blue wake. Western gulls appeared, followed the boat, and dove to pick up each piece of popcorn. In no time, there were also Heerman's gulls and California gulls following us for the corn. They would attract other birds we were told.

Soon I heard the shout, "Common murre!" and looked to see a black and white bird flying over the surface of the ocean.

"Did you get him?" someone asked.

"Yes," I replied. "A fine old saddle shoe."

I'd been waiting to say that. Murres are in the auk family, also referred to as the alcids. They are very penguin-like, though not related. Like penguins, they are black and white, and they cannot walk well as their hind feet are positioned too far to the rear, but they can fly underwater using their wings. The common murre males were often seen with a chick next to them floating on the water.

The next cry was "Sooty Shearwater!" It was a dark bird flying at great speed just inches over the surface of the rolling sea. This was as close as I would get to seeing the short-billed shearwater. The two birds are very much alike and difficult to tell apart, and the sooty is also canned and sold as a delicacy. Unfortunately, the leaders told me that the short-billed didn't generally appear off of these waters until the winter, so I would have to be content with the sooty.

The rhinoceros auklet was next. It was resting on the surface. It was a bird I had always wanted to see because of its pairs of unusual white facial plumes and the vertical spike on its bill. I could see neither because of the distance or perhaps because the bird may not have been in breeding plumage when those features are present.

When the first black-footed albatross showed up, I started muttering lines from Coleridge's Ancient Mariner. Yes, I knew it was an obvious cliché to do that and really somewhat obnoxious, but I could not help myself, and the other birders, one of whom was on his 65th trip out, seemed to expect it and happily quoted along with me. The albatross stayed with us for food or play the whole trip, and six or eight others came by and stayed too.

The black-footed albatross is kind of a goofy looking bird. When it was arching over the water with its long narrow wings, it was a marvel. When it sat on the water, however, it seemed more suitable to the barnyard. With its bulbous bill, it had a familiar look somehow—like a brown hound dog sitting contented in the living room happy to be at home.

Seeing the albatross at rest on the water gave me a clearer picture of what being a pelagic bird means. When you think of pelagic birds, you tend to assume they must either fly or drown, but the ocean is a great habitat not unlike the land to them. If the birds wish to rest, they simply sit on the water. All of them seemed to do this. The western gull, when it wasn't flying above our wake, would float on the surface. So did the little Cassin's auklet. In fact, I don't remember seeing one on the wing.

Red necked phalaropes, small pelagic sandpipers, would stream by in stringy flocks, and three species of jaegers showed up along with another shearwater, the yellow-footed.

Far offshore, we would occasionally see buoys floating in the water. They were sturdy metal contraptions each with a bell on it so that seafarers could hear them on a foggy night and not run into them. As we passed one such buoy, I looked up to see a fluttering little bird fighting against the wind. "What was this little pelagic?" I wondered. "Was it a storm-petrel?"

I heard one of the leaders behind me say, "Well, for goodness' sake!"

The little bird fought its way around the boat and finally alighted on the cabin roof. It was an immature brown-headed cowbird lost at sea miles from shore. It had been sitting on the buoy and left it for a free ride with us. I'd never seen a baby. Its breast was heavily streaked with brown. It made its way to the walkway on the side of the boat where we threw it bits of cracker. It hopped over and ate them. The cowbird would occasionally abandon ship and find itself battling the wind to catch up with us before it alighted again. Some of the birders grumbled about it. The cowbird is a pest that lays its eggs in the nests of favorite songbirds such as the warblers. They don't make their own nests. The baby cowbird that hatches is bigger and stronger than the other nestlings, and it grabs up all the food that the parents bring to the nest and in the end tips the other baby birds out. We had one of these villains in our midst, but I am particularly fond of the blackbirds and cowbirds, so I was happy to have him aboard. One of the guys mentioned that he had never seen a bronzed cowbird, and I was able to tell him about the times I had seen it.

I was looking out over the bow when I heard Debbie Shearwater screaming at the top of her lungs. "Petrel!"

Everyone ran forward and Debbie continued shouting to the skipper, "Don't stop the boat. FOLLOW THAT BIRD!"

The skipper gunned the engine, and we went after the petrel. I could see it ahead winging over the waves. We kept up with it for quite awhile. In the meantime, Debbie Shearwater was yelling, "Pictures! Take pictures!" She wanted to prove that she had got the bird. There were two guys with those cameras with long lenses attached—more like telescopes. The guys were snapping photos.

"This is why we fucking came!" Shearwater shouted.

When the bird had outdistanced us, one of the guys showed one of the pictures he had taken. I was amazed. It was a perfectly clear shot of the black and white petrel angling over the sea with its pointed wings tilted in the camera screen.

The bird was an Hawaiian petrel and was one of the very few sightings ever made near the mainland of the United States. Later, we saw Hawaiian petrels twice again, but we could not be sure if it was the same bird or not. It didn't matter, Shearwater said. It was three sightings. Not long afterwards, we got the Xantus's murrelet, which caused about the same level of excitement.

I spotted a black fin in the water and Debbie Shearwater said it was a huge shark. "It must be ten feet long," she said. The skipper told us it was a salmon shark.

I went back to the cabin. The cowbird had flown into the head, and I caught it there. It bit me, of course.

I showed it to the other birders and asked whether we should put it in a box to make sure it got to land all right.

"I think he's doing all right on his own," one of them said, so I let the bird go in the cabin, where he sat on a chair.

We spent nine hours on the water and I got fourteen life listers off the boat, and seventeen for the trip with the three I got on the beach. When we were chugging back into the harbor, I suddenly remembered the cowbird and asked if it was still aboard.

"No," one of the birders said with a smile. "When we got close to shore, he saw the land, flew off of the boat, and made a beeline for it.

I was glad to be getting back to shore myself, and I was glad the cowbird made it back to where it belonged.